# SIGNALS IN THE AIR

**Recent Titles in
the Media and Society Series**
*J. Fred MacDonald, General Editor*

# SIGNALS IN THE AIR

## Native Broadcasting in America

Michael C. Keith

Forewords by Suzan Shown Harjo and Frank Blythe
Afterword by Peggy Berryhill

Media and Society Series

Westport, Connecticut
London

**Library of Congress Cataloging-in-Publication Data**

Keith, Michael C.
    Signals in the air : native broadcasting in America / Michael C.
Keith ; forewords by Suzan Shown Harjo and Frank Blythe; afterword by Peggy
Berryhill.
        p.   cm.—(Media and society series, ISSN 0890–7161)
    Includes bibliographical references (p.   –   ) and index.
    ISBN 0–275–94876–5 (alk. paper)
    1. Indians in radio broadcasting—United States.   2. Indian radio
stations—United States.   I. Title.   II. Series.
PN1991.8.I53K45   1995
384.54′08997—dc20          94–32919

British Library Cataloguing in Publication Data is available.

Library of Congress Catalog Card Number: 94–32919
ISBN: 0–275–94876–5
ISSN: 0890–7161

First published in 1995

Praeger Publishers, 88 Post Road West, Westport, CT 06881
An imprint of Greenwood Publishing Group, Inc.

Printed in the United States of America

∞™

The paper used in this book complies with the
Permanent Paper Standard issued by the National
Information Standards Organization (Z39.48–1984).

10 9 8 7 6 5 4 3 2 1

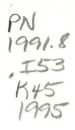
To The People who send the signals in the air

Whose voice was first sounded on this land? The voice of the red people who had but bows and arrows.

—Red Cloud, Chief, Oglala Tetons

I imagine it's been said before, and I don't claim this is an entirely new observation, but radio is a great thing.

—Will Rogers, Cherokee and humorist

# Contents

# Abbreviations

| | |
|---|---|
| AEBC | Alaska Educational Broadcasting Commission |
| AFR | Akwesasne Freedom Radio |
| AID | American Indian Development |
| AIM | American Indian Movement |
| AIPA | American Indian Press Association |
| AIROS | American Indian Radio on Satellite |
| ANSB | Alamo Navajo School Board, Inc. |
| APBC | Alaska Public Broadcasting Commission |
| APR | American Public Radio |
| APRN | Alaska Public Radio Network |
| BIA | Bureau of Indian Affairs |
| CETA | Comprehensive Employment and Training Act |
| CPB | Corporation for Public Broadcasting |
| CRTC | Canadian Radio and Television Commission |
| FCC | Federal Communications Commission |
| HUD | Housing and Urban Development |
| IBC | Indian Broadcast Center |
| ICA | Indigenous Communications Association |
| MSIP | Minority Station Improvement Program |
| NAB | National Association of Broadcasters |
| NAJA | Native American Journalist Association |

| NAPBC | Native American Public Broadcasting Consortium |
|-------|-----------------------------------------------|
| NCA   | National Congress of American Indians |
| NFCB  | National Federation of Community Broadcasters |
| NPPAG | National Program and Production Acquisition Grant |
| NPR   | National Public Radio |
| NTIA  | National Telecommunications Information Agency |
| OTA   | Office of Technology Assessment |
| PBS   | Public Broadcasting Service |
| PTFP  | Public Telecommunications Facilities Program |
| SRN   | Superior Radio Network |

# Foreword

by Suzan Shown Harjo

Suzan Shown Harjo is president of the Morning Star Institute, founding co-chair of the Howard Simons Fund for Indian journalists, founding trustee of the National Museum of the American Indian, a poet and writer, and a veteran of Native radio broadcasting.

The proliferation of Native American voices on radios throughout Indian country is a source of great familial and collegial pride. In the early days of the American Indian Press Association (AIPA), those of us who lived and breathed broadcast journalism and production could have met in an edit booth. Indian radio stations and programs in the United States were few in number, and the handful of Native managers and programmers were all too familiar with the wolf at the door.

At that time, during the late 1960s and early 1970s, many tribal leaders were skeptical about the value of tribally sponsored radio and Indian programming on radio in general. In a world where tribal ships of state were captained by the Bureau of Indian Affairs (BIA) and many Native peoples were content just sailing down the mainstream, the medium was viewed as a vehicle for Indian activism—a voice that stirred factionalism and threatened the order of the day at home with talk of political injustice and demands for Indian religious freedom and sovereign treaty rights.

The messages of ancient visions and respect for Mother Earth, natural law, and human rights resonated (then as now) in an America searching for cultural identity, for political thought and ideology that could be trusted, for ways of getting through life without killing one another or the planet. The airwaves amplified the messages of those who were voiceless at home and in the reservation border towns and in the streets of the Indian relocation cities. The messengers—traditional elders, spiritual leaders, grass-roots tribal people, warriors from the fishing and land struggles, and those freshly wounded from alcoholism, prisons and Vietnam—were targeted by the federal government and its "good Indians" for surveillance, character assassination, and investigation as domestic terrorists, destroyers of property, and worse. Most of the Indian broadcasters, like some of the Indian educators and tribal leaders who promoted or espoused those messages, did not escape being shot along with the messengers, occasionally as a less than apocryphal proposition.

Native peoples were drawn to broadcasting, irrespective of the few outlets at home and the limited opportunities in commercial radio and television. The draw was an audience and, in the case of radio, the natural transition of Indian oral history and storytelling traditions.

Native broadcasters, most of whom grew up with rock and roll and radio talk-jocks, gravitated to public broadcasting, or listener-sponsored radio, mainly because that was where the jobs were and because commercial radio did not accommodate a story told from beginning to end or a news report that buried the lead or "dead air." In Native programming and over the airwaves of Indian stations, there is a traditional rhythm that values the poetry of silence for punctuation and completion of thought—silence that is listener-friendly and invites reflective moments and sets up the point of the story or the turn-about humor at the end. This cadence—now recognized in part as a Charles Kuralt or Bill Moyers style on television—originated in radio of that time in programs produced by Native people.

My own life in radio began in New York City, where I had moved from Oklahoma to Greenwich Village to write and work in theater and politics. As a young mother with a lot of time at home, I found radio a lifeline that stimulated thought and provided grown-up companionship without commanding total attention. My favorite station was WBAI–FM, which was the standard bearer for free speech, alternative news, and cutting-edge arts and political views programming. While there was some reporting of news about Indians, the listeners in the six-state area reached by the station were missing the Indian story on the very best of progressive radio. Native peoples' issues and social movements were as absent on the radio as they were in the classrooms and in recorded history. This absence was ironic given that Native music, worldviews, and words were present throughout American popular culture, providing context, inspiration, symbology, and validation for environmental and political movements, alternative lifestyles, clothing, and the arts.

Over the years, broadcasting has offered a wide variety of opportunities for Native people (young and not-so-young) to develop and refine their myriad skills, particularly at smaller stations. It would be difficult for an individual to work in any one aspect of broadcasting without gaining at least a little experience in another aspect.

Radio can be a booster of self-esteem because of its collaborative (reinforcing) context and the acknowledgement that is derived from meaningful audience response to good programming. Studio efforts can have an impact on the lives of Native peoples. For those whose focus is programming, there is no better medium than Native-owned stations for the communitywide promotion of Indian culture, history, art, philosophy, and education. There is no more inclusive, effective, and empowering form of communication for Native peoples.

Native-owned stations are ideal for the revitalization and preservation of Indigenous languages and for the presentation and documentation of oral history and storytelling. However, Native radio and television stations face formidable funding problems and control issues—that is, how to obtain the money needed to survive and who decides what is aired? In addition, Native stations face ethical issues that arise in connection with cultural appropriateness, traditional religious tenets, and tribal policy and politics. For stations that are tribally owned and controlled, there exists the same tension that National Public Radio (NPR) faces with its federal sponsor, which in some ways is not all that different from corporate-owned and -controlled radio and commercial stations. As more stations are owned and controlled by Native individuals, rather than by tribal governments, the tensions will shift in kind but not in degree.

Native radio will continue to be the primary source of information and entertainment for most Indian people for a good long time to come. It is affordable and accessible for those who are often politically disenfranchised, for the elderly and infirm who cannot participate in community events in person, and for those who work in the home and elsewhere who need a medium that does not require the use of the hands or eye contact. It is accessible also for those who can only receive instruction and follow a course at home, for those who have no means of reaching cultural activities, and for those who do not read or who have no computers or satellite dishes.

Native "signals in the air" help create cultural and societal cohesion and are a bridge between Native and non-Native peoples, between preindustrially based and technologically based societies. The value of this bridge is incalculable.

# Foreword ■

## by Frank Blythe

Frank Blythe is founding member and executive director of the Native American Public Broadcasting Consortium, codirector of the American Indian Radio on Satellite Project, and co-chair of the Native Communications Group. He is a former broadcaster and producer.

"Are Indian radio stations allowed to play country music instead of classical?" That was asked of me during a visit to WOJB–FM in Lac Court Oreilles Reservation, Wisconsin, in 1981. I was there to discuss plans for a Native radio satellite network. In 1994 that same station was one of twenty–five Native American radio stations to broadcast "Live from the White House," an historic tribal nations-to-nations meeting with the president of the United States on American Indian Radio on Satellite (AIROS).

In the intervening thirteen years between my visit and that landmark broadcast, Native radio came into its own. As a growing medium learning to use its collective voice, it has evolved from one station in 1971 to more than two dozen public and commercial stations today. Native broadcasting has its own national satellite network and has acquired the political leverage to garner more financial support because of the impact it has in the Indigenous community. On the reservation it is the sole source for Indian news, as well as the preserver of Native language and culture. It all adds up to Native American empowerment to produce, program, and distribute what is important to Indigenous community, instead of the community's being force-fed news and information from unconcerned mainstream media.

As head of the Native American Public Broadcasting Consortium (NAPBC), I have been involved (either directly or indirectly) in the journey from "smoke signals to satellite," which was the title of the 1981 satellite-planning study conducted by my consortium and a team of consultants. Since the cost of satellite technology was greater back then than it is today, the dream of a Native radio community remained just that until recently. Many questions were raised before this dream was realized. For example, who will use the satellite? What will be carried on it? How will stations afford it? And, reminiscent of the question presented me at WOJB, Are Indians allowed to have their own satellite system? The answer to the last question was yes! A thousand times yes! And AIROS is living proof of that. Getting the bird up required the formidable efforts of the NAPBC and ICA (Indigenous Communications Association) and the financial support from the Corporation of Public Broadcasting (CPB).

*Signals in the Air* retraces this smoke signals-to-satellite story including many of the principals who made it happen and who are taking Native electronic media onto the much heralded information superhighway. This book is a significant achievement and a welcome addition to the small list of publications on this subject. It gives those of us who work in the field a chance to see where we have come from and an opportunity to reflect on where we are headed.

Tribal America is building more radio stations, and AIROS is ready to bring voices from these stations to national public radio audiences and the world.

# Preface

The history of Native Americans is a familiar and sad one. No group of people has endured more hardship and tragedy. Their losses are unparalleled in history. What was theirs was taken from them—a land, a way of life. But while they have suffered and sometimes fallen, they have not perished. Their survival is a tribute to the audacious spirit that is at the core of the American Indian, and Native broadcast stations stand as modern symbols of this will to abide.

In remote stretches of plain, tundra, and desert, radio antennas rise skyward, radiating their unique signals to the inhabitants of these austere landscapes—the nation's Indigenous people.

It was on one such stretch of desolate ground that 300 Sioux Indians were massacred by U.S. cavalry during the last decade of the nineteenth century, the same decade in which Marconi introduced his wireless telegraph. That such disparate events—one a poignant example of man's inhumanity toward man and the other a great leap forward in human communications—could occupy the same tract of chronology seems more than a little ironic. Wounded Knee and radio, odd calendar mates indeed.

Equally odd to some in present-day mainstream society is the existence of broadcast stations that program exclusively for Indians. Yet more than two dozen broadcast frequencies are operated by Native Americans for Native Americans.

Indian policy expert Francis Prucha views the presence of Indigenous electronic media as "an increasing accommodation of the Indians to white technology." While this statement may suggest a Native concession to the dominant Anglo culture, it also points to a growing awareness by Natives of the value of media within their own world.

Native-operated broadcast stations are largely the result of a move away from Indian assimilation of white people's ways (a government policy during the first half of the century) toward a plan for self-determination and cultural preservation.

In the late 1960s and early 1970s, as the quest for equality by minority groups reached full velocity, Indians rejected the notion of abandoning their rich heritage and tradition for the purpose of blending into the ascendant culture. Rather than absorbing the contents of mainstream electronic media, the aim of Native American radio and television was to preserve a culture and prevent its possible extinction. Broadcasting was and is viewed as a means for survival and empowerment by members of the Indigenous community. Its raison d'être is not monetary gain but profit of a much rarer nature.

Employing a microphone was a natural step for a culture with a rich oral tradition, a culture whose identity has always been conveyed through language. Electronic media simply provided a modern means for sustaining this tradition. Long before there was radio, television, or books, storytelling was used to teach Native children and adults about life and the past.

Native media are not a recent manifestation. The first Indian newspaper, the *Cherokee Phoenix*, appeared in 1828, nearly a century and a half ahead of the first Native-operated broadcast station. Yet while the Native press proliferated in various forms in the United States, the birth of Indigenous electronic media was belated. Their evolution has been slow, especially in contrast to Canada, where government support has been far more substantial.

Nonetheless, Native Americans have harnessed the airwaves. The past two decades have witnessed the growth of a truly unique medium, one that now employs satellite technology to beam Native programming to both the Indigenous stations of the United States and the world. Today Indian broadcasters are charting their routes on the information highway. They are the new *eyapaha* (Lakota word for "voice" or "town crier").

*Signals in the Air* is the first book-length study of Native broadcasting in America, and as such it will likely raise more questions than it answers. It is the author's hope that this first attempt will inspire even more detailed studies of this extraordinary subject.

This story could not have been adequately told without the contributions of many individuals. Foremost among them are Ray Cook (Mohawk) and Joseph Orozco (Hupa). They have been my true collaborators and partners in this endeavor. Their guidance, knowledge, and compassion inform nearly every page of this work.

The studies of Bruce Smith and Jerry Brigham, and James E. Murphy and Sharon M. Murphy served as essential road maps during the planning stage of the book, and their subsequent contributions have enriched several chapters. They were among the very first to publish articles and chapters on Native American broadcasting. Their trailblazing gave light to the path this book has followed.

More than anything, this book has relied on the perspectives of the country's Native broadcasters and producers. It is their voice that moves the narrative and comprises its heart. They tell their own story here, which rightfully earns them acknowledgment as the book's coauthors. It is to them that this book is dedicated.

A debt of gratitude is owed the following individuals for their significant contributions and assistance: Rose Robinson, Charles Trimble, Mary Dinota, E. B. Eiselein, Nan Rubin, Frank Blythe, Suzan Shown Harjo, Peggy Berryhill, Karen Holp, Jay Williams, Jr., Dwight Ellis, Joseph Gill, S. J., Francis Prucha, S. J., Michael Goldberg, Allen Myers, Wayne Bundy, Lynn Chadwick, Corey Flintoff, Susan Braine, Tom Thomas, Keith Winsell, Vernon Bellecourt, Richard Harland, Mark Tilsen, and Dale Means.

Special thanks are due to my colleagues at Boston College, whose support and goodwill made doing this book possible. A hearty tip of the hat goes to John Katsulas for his Nexus search on the topic.

Precious suggestions and advice were made by my friends and manuscript readers, Robert Hilliard and Lindy Bonczek. I am deeply indebted to them for their limitless kindness and generosity.

A heartfelt word of appreciation is owed to my wife and family for their exceptional tolerance and understanding during the days of this book's gestation.

Miigwetch!!

## Chapter One

# Murmurs to Metawce: Early Native Broadcasts

Give ear. I am the mouth of my nation. When you listen to me, you listen to all Iroquois. There is no evil in my heart. My song is the song of peace.

—Kiosaton, Iroquois Chief,
September 1645

## THE INDIGENOUS POPULATION

While American Indian broadcast station signals cover less than a sixth of the United States land mass, the Indigenous population itself is widespread. The nation's 2 million Native Americans (0.8 percent of the U.S. population) live everywhere, not just on reservations, as many non-Indians assume. In fact, the majority of Indigenous people reside off reservations in both rural and urban settings. "While it is a common stereotype to think of Indians as a rural people living on remote reservations, the fact is that there has been a migration to the cities,"[1] observes Native researcher E. B. Eiselein, who adds that by the 1980s more than 50 percent of the Native population resided in cities. In 1990 the metropolitan areas of Los Angeles, New York City, Tulsa, Oklahoma City, and Tucson had a combined Native population of over a quarter million.

*Metawce* is the Virginia Indian term for "ears."

The second largest segment of the Native population, however, may be found on the country's 300 reservations, which are located in thirty-three states and cover 55 million acres.

These range from large reservations such as Navajo in Arizona, New Mexico, Colorado, and Utah (nearly 15 million acres) and Tohono O'odham (nearly 3 million acres) to reservations of less than one acre such as the Sheep Ranch Rancheria near Sacramento, California. Due to federal policies such as the Dawes Act[2], which attempted to destroy tribal land ownership, only 45 percent of the land within reservation boundaries is actually owned by the tribes.[3]

Indian land and communities (not necessarily reservations) are scattered throughout the country. States with the most significant number of Native Americans include South Dakota, Minnesota, South Carolina, Montana, Iowa, California, Oregon, Arizona, Oklahoma, North Dakota, Washington, Wisconsin, New Mexico, Virginia, New York, Idaho, Kansas, North Carolina, Mississippi, Colorado, Wyoming, Utah, Louisiana, and Alaska. Alaska has more than 200 Native communities, and Oklahoma, New Mexico, Oregon, Wisconsin, Arizona, Nevada, and California each have a dozen or more. Oklahoma, California, Arizona, and New Mexico alone account for nearly half of the country's Native population. States with the fewest Indians include Vermont, Delaware, and New Hampshire. However, there are still nearly 2,000 Native Americans living in each of these states.[4] There are a dozen states with no prominent Native enclaves.

There are 547 federally recognized tribes in the United States, an indication of the diversity that exists within Native American culture. "Natives are not a homogeneous population. Dozens of Native languages are spoken in the United States. . . . Natives also maintain diverse life styles. In rural and especially northern areas, many still subsist by hunting and gathering. Others have settled comfortably into urban areas and have entered mainstream Canadian and American life."[5]

American Indians have often been perceived as one ethnic group by Anglo society, but this is a misconception. "References to Indian Culture or Indian People as a single cultural entity are both misleading and false. Historically, there were several hundred Indian cultures in what is now the United States. These cultures varied greatly from agricultural peoples . . . to nomadic hunters and gatherers. The experiences and world-view of an Iroquois from New York are culturally different from that of a Makah from Washington."[6]

Tribes are widely distributed throughout the country. For example, in what is referred to as the Eastern Woodlands may be found the Iroquois, Mohegan, Delaware, and Shawnee tribes, while the Southeast is home to the Seminole, Choctaw, Cherokee, and Creek tribes. In the Great Plains reside the Sioux, Pawnee, Arapaho, Ponca, and Cheyenne, and in the West and Southwest live the Apache, Navajo, Ute, Shoshoni, Hupa, and Paiute. Dozens of other lesser known tribes also call these various regions home.

In part, Native American cultural diversity and population diffusion have inhibited the expansion of Native electronic media services. The abject social and economic climate in much of Native America has impeded growth in this area as well. The poorest county in the United States (Shannon, South Dakota) is Native American. There 63.1 percent of the population live below the national poverty level. Unemployment is over 30 percent on several reservations (Fort Apache, Pine Ridge, Navajo, Rosebud). The jobless rate is highest among Sioux, Apache, and Navajo.[7]

With few exceptions, money simply has not been available to create Native broadcast stations or programming. Compared with mainstream America, Native Americans residing on reservations receive significantly poorer-quality education and have less access to economic resources, although great pockets of wealth do exist in some Indian communities.

## BROADCASTS FOR NATIVES

Despite radio's auspicious arrival and astronomic rise to prominence in the 1920s and 1930s (and virtual ubiquity by World War II), Native Americans were essentially left unserved and ignored by broadcasters. That remained pretty much the case until they established their own electronic media in the 1970s.

Ray Cook, executive director of the Indigenous Communications Association, makes this observation:

In the United States there were no attempts by mainstream commercial radio to produce programs for Native audiences. Let me clarify this by saying that if you're looking for programs that were produced to empower Native communities to help them achieve control over their own destinies and realities, I can safely say that before 1972, when Native broadcasting was launched with the first Indian owned and operated station going on the air, there were no efforts to provide sustaining programming anywhere in the U.S. That is, nothing that served the needs of Indigenous people, or for that matter even entertained them.[8]

Native American Public Broadcasting Consortium (NAPBC) director Frank Blythe concurs with Cook that programs focusing on Indian society and culture were a rarity during radio's much touted golden age and were no more in evidence in the 1950s, when a shift to more local program origination occurred. "You know, I just can't recall hearing of anything much before the 1960's. It just wasn't there, or if it was it was an isolated phenomenon."[9]

When recalling his youth in the 1930s, prominent Native journalist Tim Giago has memories of white sporting events and Anglo songs, such as "Somewhere over the Rainbow" and "The Blue Ridge Mountains of Virginia," filling the airwaves over his reservation.

In his 1980 study on ethnic broadcasting, Theodore Grame indicates the paucity of Native programming in the United States prior to World War II. "In 1943 there seems to have been only one such broadcast in the nation, over WNAD in Norman, Oklahoma."[10]

The climate began to change somewhat during the 1960s as the nation's dominant Anglo culture had its ethnic sensibilities aroused by the call for equality by minority groups, including Native Americans. An atmosphere of greater receptivity and interest in Indigenous programming by mainstream broadcasters was one result of the human rights movement.

However, during the decades leading up to this shift in attitudes, Native Americans had little relationship with the nation's growing electronic media industry, and in areas unserved by Native-owned and -operated broadcast stations, the situation remains much the same today. For example, the quarter million Native Americans living in Oklahoma have no broadcast media of their own and are only modestly served by the state's electronic media. "Natives aren't getting much attention from broadcasters in this state. There is very little on either commercial or noncommercial stations on a weekly basis here, which may seem rather surprising considering that this state has a major Indian population,"[11] says Karen Holp, general manager of Oklahoma public broadcast stations KGOU and KROU.

Holp believes that the scattered nature of the Indigenous population in Oklahoma has had an effect on the level of broadcast service to this group.

Natives are so spread across the state that this has a twofold impact. For one thing, it has kept the creation of Native-owned and -operated stations from happening, because the thinking is that there aren't enough potential listeners to constitute a viable audience for a station, unless the station covers the entire state. Secondly, established stations don't perceive a thick enough market to justify dedicating regular programming. A series or feature here and there, yes, but ongoing programming, rarely.[12]

Do Oklahoma Native Americans perceive the shortage of service by the state's broadcasters as having an impact on them? Yes, says Bob Harmon, economic development director for the Kaw Nation of Oklahoma. "Area tribes currently communicate to their members through a tribal newspaper, which is only published quarterly, and a local paper announces meetings. Radio or television would be more immediate forms of media for getting information out, plus they would be there constantly to remind Indians and non-Indians alike that there is an Indian presence and culture in the area."[13]

Harmon and other Native Americans would like to see Native electronic media developed in their state.

Many of us believe a Native owned and operated station could definitely provide a special service to the state's Indian communities. Whether the broadcast was for profit or non-commercial, the local Indian tribes could benefit their members by providing information, such as where to pick up food commodities, when meetings are to be held, what other tribes are doing, and so on. Programs regarding tribal culture could also be aired so as to instill pride and knowledge among tribal members. If the broadcast station was commercial, tribes could promote their gaming enterprises, smokeshops, and other businesses over the air.[14]

Despite the attitude of many Oklahoma Indians that it would be a good idea to establish their own electronic media, to date proposals to bring this about have failed, as have similar attempts in other states without Native broadcasting outlets.

In Nebraska, another state with no Native broadcast media and a large Indigenous population, there have been plans over the years to create stations, but to date nothing has happened. Deborah Wright, chairwoman of the Ponca tribe of Nebraska, says that while a Native station would benefit her tribe, there are no intentions to build one. "We're not planning on any. But I can see the value in having one. A Native American station would be beneficial as information across the radio waves to members would better the communication levels. Also a station would enhance the appreciation of Native American sensitivity and spirituality."[15]

The Indigenous Communications Association (ICA) predicts that it is only a matter of time before most states with substantial Native populations have Indian-operated broadcast stations. "This is going to happen. Exactly when is hard to predict, but I would say within the next decade or so. The climate for this to occur is improving rapidly, due to a number of factors. One is when Natives are tired of being in the dark, constantly subject to another culture's interpretations of the world,"[16] says Ray Cook.

Meanwhile, many Native Americans go unserved even in those states with Indian-run stations. Often Native people and communities exist in remote locales and therefore are beyond the reach of indigenous broadcast signals. For example, owing to the great size of Alaska, the majority of its Indigenous residents do not receive Native broadcasts, or, for that matter, broadcasts of any kind.

The villages of Yakutat and Andreafshi are representative of the situation in extreme remote areas. Although located in different regions of Alaska, their experiences are similar. "We don't receive any Native broadcast stations here. Either we are too far or the signals are just too weak to reach us,"[17] says Andreakshi's administrator, Deborah Alstrom.

The executive director of the Yakutat Native Association, Nellie Vale, says there is little for people in her village to tune to. "We don't have access to Native stations here in Yakutat. There aren't many in Alaska to begin with, and our location 300 miles north of Juneau and 500 miles south of Anchorage prohibits us from picking up stations easily. The only radio station here is a religious station that operates by satellite. We get some Native news on the Rural Alaska Network TV station, but only on Sunday night. That's it where we are."[18]

Most mainstream stations whose signals do reach large numbers of Indians do not direct programming to them. A case in point is KKOB–AM, which has been broadcasting in New Mexico since 1922. "We cover two thirds of the state, but we keep our programming mainstream. We don't air Native features per se. I think that has been pretty much the case since the station began operating,"[19] says the station's general manager, Jim Pidrock.

According to *Broadcasting and Cable Yearbook*'s listing of stations in South Dakota (one of the country's major Indigenous centers), only one commercial station there offers Native programming, although nationally ninety-two stations indicate some type of weekly programming (typically one to three hours) for Indians.[20]

The state with the greatest number of radio stations offering programming to Natives is Alaska, with fourteen. Oklahoma, the state with the largest Native population, has eight stations airing regular Indigenous features. California and Arizona have six stations apiece broadcasting Native programs, while New Mexico has nine.

In 1994 there were 11,577 radio stations, 1,518 television stations, 11,385 cable systems, and 1,456 low-power television (LPTV) operations in America.[21] Of these totals, just over two dozen radio stations and under a half dozen LPTVs were licensed to Native Americans (mostly educational institutions) and were directing their programming to that audience.[22]

## NATIVE PROGRAMMING ON NON-NATIVE STATIONS

Although more the exception than the rule, programs containing topics relevant to the Native American experience have been aired nearly since radio's inception. However, regularly scheduled programs for Indians were virtually nonexistent in the early days of broadcasting. Sustaining broadcasts with Native themes by the major networks were nowhere to be found. Since advertisers were interested in reaching large audiences with great buying power, Indians were virtually ignored by the national broadcast conglomerates.

In the United States and Alaska there were only "varying amounts of Native-oriented programming on white-owned stations."[23] Thus, Natives were left with little alternative but to tune to mainstream signals, if they could pick them up. "Because many Natives live in rural areas, they often listened to high powered AM radio signals originating from distant urban areas."[24]

If stations broadcasting in areas with substantial numbers of Indians were disinclined to offer programs tailored for them, they found it in their hearts to craft commercial messages for their consumption, observes ICA's Cook:

Many Anglo stations in places with large Native populations, like Minneapolis, San Francisco, Gallup, and Oklahoma City—places near oil and coal rich tribes, have targeted the pocketbooks of Indians. These stations would air commercials, sometimes in the local Native language, so when the monthly or biweekly checks would come in the Indians would have information on which to base purchases. That was the extent of Native-oriented programming designed for Indian consumption by a lot of these mainstream stations.[25]

Public-affairs programming obligations as established by the Federal Communications Commission (FCC) have been and remain a prime motivator behind many mainstream broadcasts of occasional or regularly scheduled Indian-oriented programs. "To fulfill our Public Affairs commitment, we air a regular weekly Indian program called 'Native America Speaks'[26] every Sunday from 5:30 to 6:00 A.M. This and other Public Affairs oriented Native programs have been broadcast since the early days of the station, which went on the air back in the 1920's. We're a 50,000 watt station that covers a large part of the western U.S.,"[27] observes Oklahoma City station KOMA–AM's administrator, Mary Murdock.

KGFF–AM, another Oklahoma station, provides programming for Natives as part of its ongoing public service commitment. Says the station's operations and program manager, Michael Askins:

We have a station obligation to provide news and public service to the various Native Nations that are within our signal area. Over the years we aired two specific programs. One was *The First Indian Baptist Church of Shawnee,* which ran throughout the 1980's. It was a sponsored weekly program that featured Christian doctrine aimed at Native Americans and the issues that face them in daily life. This program was multilingual, meaning that various segments were in the language of area Nations (Seminole, Shawnee, Potawatomie, Creek, Kickapoo, and so on). The second program was *Muskogee Nation News,* which was produced by the Creek Nation and aired weekly as a public service program. Our coverage of news and special events within the Creek Nation won a public service award from that tribe in 1992. The program aired on our station in the early 1990's until it went out of production. Should the Creek Nation restore production of this program, KGFF wouldn't hesitate to schedule it.[28]

Station KTLQ in Tulsa also has lent its airwaves to various tribes that provide the station with tapes, says general manager Martha Demaree. "We aired Creek and Cherokee Nation programs on Sunday mornings, until we stopped receiving their tapes. We'd be more than willing to resume this service, if they're interested. We also work with the Cherokee Nation to promote drug awareness. We air a program on this topic one Sunday per month. They come to the studio and produce the program."[29]

Typically, Native programs on Anglo stations are in the form of information soundbites or half-hour features. Notes KYNT's operations manager, Scott Kooistra:

Here in Yankton we do attempt to meet some of the needs of our local Indian population. On our talk segments, we address topics related to Native American issues and air short as well as lengthy pieces. In the past year, we have aired a talk show featuring a chief who discussed story-telling and hoop dancing. We did a show during Native American week, which has replaced Columbus Day in South Dakota. We aired another program featuring Native Americans at our human resource center, and recently we interviewed a tribal leader about a new Indian casino built just southwest of Yankton.[30]

As stated earlier, in Alaska more Native Americans are reached by Indian-operated radio stations than in any other state. At the same time, broadcast service directed to indigenous people by mainstream stations is also higher there than in most states. Stations such as KNOM and KICY in Nome and KCAM in Glennallen have traditionally devoted significant segments of their on-air schedules to Natives. These and many other non-Indian stations in Alaska have a religious (Christian) orientation. Station manager George Reichman tells of his station's programming slant:

At KCAM we currently air *Native Pastor* from 1:00 to 1:30 on Sunday afternoons. These preaching programs were recorded by the Athabascan Indian pastors in our listening area. From 1:30 to 1:45 Sundays we air *Crosswinds,* a program of Indian and Eskimo singing and giving ceremonies. It is recorded about 140 miles from here but sometimes features Native individuals and groups from our area. Also we're presently airing *Indian Bible Hour* on Sunday afternoons. It is a Canadian program featuring Native Americans from Canada singing and preaching. Over the years, we've aired many Native programs, the majority of which were produced outside the station.[31]

There have been very few instances of stations licensed to non-Indians that program exclusively to Native Americans.[32] One such station is KNDN in Farmington, New Mexico. It is staffed by Navajos, who oversee all aspects of operation, including production and programming. Its slogan is "All Navajo, All the Time." Says Dale Felkner, the station's general manager,

We serve approximately half of the population of the Navajo Indian reservation, the largest of all U.S. reservations. A total land mass of 25 thousand square miles. KNDN serves about one-half the land area and one-half the population. All program elements—news, commercials, features—are done in Native tongue. . . . Some radio stations that "ring" the reservation offer one to three hours daily Navajo programming. . . . Stations in Gallup, Flagstaff, Holbrooks, and Cortez block out portions of certain dayparts for the Navajo listener, but KNDN does so around the clock. We're pure-blood.[33]

Arizona is also home for KHAC–AM, licensed to Western Indian Ministries, which programs organized religion for Navajos and Hopis. "Our mission is to tell area Natives about Christianity. We have programs in English and Indian to share the Gospel of Jesus Christ. We also broadcast regular information features, like news and weather, to the Indigenous community within our signal area,"[34] states the manager, Jim Maiorano.

Other commercial stations in the Southwest have targeted the Navajo market with their broadcasts. In the 1970s KCLS in Flagstaff, Arizona, aired *Navajo County Time* daily from 5 to 6 A.M., which made it especially appealing to ranchers who were up before dawn tending their livestock. The program featured country music (a favorite form of music to many Indians), news, and local announcements of special interest to its audience.[35] During the 1950s, Gallup, New Mexico, station KGAK presented programming in Navajo that also focused on music, news, and community events. Both stations found such programming to be commercially viable.[36]

Another Gallup station, KYVA-AM, also found that revenue could be generated by airing Navajo features. As far back as the 1950s, the station has aired sponsored programs of news and music designed for local Indian tastes.

Ironically, but perhaps understandably from an entrepreneurial point of view, the amount of Indigenous programming on mainstream stations has decreased in areas served by Native-operated stations.

In the 1970s and 1980s the Navajo Film and Media Commission produced *Navajo Nation Report* for television. It was picked up by several mainstream stations in the southwest, primarily in Arizona and New Mexico.[37]

Over the years, much of the Native programming on mainstream stations has been produced by Indians. Native producer Peggy Berryhill contends that there is a history of Indian involvement in radio, even if the amount of Native programming in mainstream broadcasting has been nominal. "Indians have been there. Before there were Native stations, there were Native programs and Native broadcasters. These people helped open the doors for Native stations."[38]

## NATIVE PROGRAMMING ON PUBLIC STATIONS

The majority of Native programs are produced and broadcast by noncommercial public stations. Because they have been less concerned about ratings and advertisers, they have developed a more altruistic program catalog.

Prior to 1950, as well as after, some colleges and universities (particularly in the Dakotas and Southwest) occasionally produced programs with Native content for educational broadcasts, but with the conception of Pacifica Radio in 1949 at KPFA in Berkeley, California, the opportunities for Native producers improved.

Pacifica's unique commitment to the unconventional and innovative and its distinctly nonconformist (if not antiestablishment) posture provided entrée to the airwaves for many would-be Native broadcasters, such as Frank Ray Harjo and Suzan Shown Harjo, who would regularly produce pieces (such as "Seeing Red") related to Indians in the 1960s and 1970s for Pacifica stations in New York, San Francisco, Los Angeles, Dallas, and Washington, D.C.

Included among Pacifica's most notable Native programs are the 1961 documentary "The Angry Indians," aired over WBAI; 1970s programs on AIM, such as "Native American Spirtual Values" and "The American Indian

Movement"; issue-based features such as "American Indians and Racism," "In the Beginning: A Native American Woman's View," "Sisters and Allies," and "Free the People: The Case of Leonard Peltier"; and an eight-part documentary on a Shoshone medicine man.

Over the decades, Pacifica stations have remained a bastion for Native programming, with shows such as *Living on Indian Time*, which has aired over KPFA for more than twenty years. It is broadcast to listeners in the San Francisco Bay area every Friday night between eight and nine and is considered a vital voice for Indians in the area. "The program's focus changes depending on the individuals involved, but it invariably deals with community issues relevant to the Native American experience."[39]

The emergence in 1970 of taxpayer-supported public broadcasting pushed the door open even wider for Native producers and programs for and about Indigenous people. Countless features containing Indian subject matter have been aired by Public Broadcasting Service (PBS) television stations and National Public Radio (NPR) affiliates in the twenty-five years of their existence. Observes Ray Cook on the inauguration of public broadcasting:

This was a turning point certainly. Reflecting on this, I recall that somewhere between 1970 and 1975 a Mohawk fellow by the name of Louis Cook worked for *Akwesasne Notes* and put together tapes of talks and major events that took place around the Iroquois territory. He would submit his work to NPR. He had someplace to go with it. This was an important change. The goal of his programs was to educate the non-Indian about the issues facing Indians. People like Cook, Trudell, Harjo, and later Berryhill, were the broadcast pioneers who got the word out about Native struggles. Their programs on Public radio increased the audience's understanding of Native people. It was real valid work.[40]

The market for Native programs was enhanced yet again when American Public Radio (known today as Public Radio International) came on the scene in 1983. Both APR and NPR function primarily as program distributors. Production typically occurs independent of the networks, often at local affiliate stations or government and public service organizations.

In 1992 APR offered its member stations a thirteen-part series called *Spirits of the Present: The Legacy from Native America*. Highly praised by listeners and critics, it was produced by Radio Smithsonian, which has prepared other programs on Native America.

NPR reported no distribution of Native programs at the end of 1993. "We have no nationally distributed programs exclusively Native American in orientation. We used to distribute *National Native News*, but it's now over at American Public Radio. Some of our documentaries, such as *Horizon* and *Sound Print*, devote segments to Native themes, but only occasionally. *Morning Edition* and *All Things Considered* have aired Native American feature stories."[41]

PBS has televised several documentary-type features on aspects of Indian life. These programs too have been produced largely by affiliate stations and independent producers, who typically work with grant money provided by the Corporation of Public Broadcasting, as well as other government agencies and public-service organizations.

A significant stride forward in the development of Native broadcasting took place in 1987 with the launching of *National Native News* on 30 stations. This satellite-delivered ten-minute news update is offered daily from the Alaska Public Radio Network in Anchorage. What makes this program unique is that its signal can potentially reach the majority of Native Americans. Award-winning *National Native News* is distributed to more than 400 public radio stations and carried by 170. The broadcast is divided between top news stories that affect Native Americans and more in-depth features. Until 1994 it was hosted by Gary Fife, whose name became a household word in the Indian community.

A measure of the program's significance was the perservation of its broadcasts in an archive in 1993 by the Smithsonian's National Museum of the American Indian. Observed Gary Fife on this occasion,

This is the first time any institution has ever taken a real good, hard look at the contemporary affairs of Native people. Death and destruction characterizes most of the [white] media coverage of Native news. . . . Or dueling cameras at dance festivals. That's okay as far as it goes, but the old beads- and-feathers story just isn't enough anymore. . . . Education budgets, housing, economic development and gaming, the sobriety movement. These are the real stories of Native America.[42]

Many Native-operated radio stations repeat the daily broadcast of *National Native News*, attesting to the value placed upon this first-ever, countrywide Indian news report. KMHA radio on the Fort Berthold reservation in North Dakota airs the program five times a day. The broadcast "has been a real breakthrough for reservations that tend to be isolated and tend to be like a large extended family that doesn't get involved in what's going on in other areas."[43]

Several new Native programs have recently surfaced on public radio stations. One is a new series called *Creative Tracks*: *Native American Artists in the 90s*. "The four one-half hour documentaries and six modules were produced by WSLU in Canton, New York. The series was made available to stations subscribing to NPR's Cultural Programming Service and also was made available to Native stations."[44]

Native producer Peggy Berryhill has created a new magazine program for radio called *Indigenous Voices.* It is to be principally produced with submissions from tribal stations from which Berryhill also draws her cohosts. The idea behind this approach is to share the voices of Native radio stations with the rest of the listening community around the country. The program was launched with a start-up grant from the Corporation for Public Broadcasting (CPB) and is a Native American Public Broadcasting Consortium (NAPBC) project. It is to be distributed by AIROS, a new, Native communication satellite service.

For obvious reasons, in-house production activity devoted to Native programming is most prevalent at public radio stations whose signals reach large, local Indigenous populations. KANW–FM in Albuquerque is representative. The station's program director, Leigh-Ann M. Gerow, relates the following:

We have two programs aimed at Native American audiences. The first is called *Echoes of the Native American.* It is a weekly, 15 minute feature which is repeated once. The program is hosted by a representative of the Indian Affairs office of the Albuquerque Public School board, and it is largely aimed at students in the primary grades. It airs at 10 A.M. Tuesdays and at 2:30 P.M. on Thursdays. The content includes announcements of upcoming events sponsored by the office, interviews with Indian artisans and musicians, and stories relating to Native holiday traditions. It airs during the school year (September through May). The second program is an adult-oriented music show that airs Thursday evenings. The local host, Beulah Sunrise, opens the show each week with APRN's *National Native News*, then follows with a variety of music. The mix is approximately 50 percent Native, 25 percent Country, and 25 percent rock. Beulah also makes regular announcements about upcoming powwows, and sometimes she will interview powwow or rodeo participants. Both of these programs have been on KANW for years, at least since the early 1970's. Of course, the hosts have changed, but the shows have remained pretty much the same. Every so often there will be a local underwriter for the evening music show, but otherwise they are not sponsored. We also carry specials by APR when they are made available. The past years we were able to air "A Song for Wounded Knee" and the "World Cafe" special for Indigenous People's Day.[45]

California public radio stations are among the most active in generating Native programming. KKUP in Cupertino, KPOO in San Francisco, KMUD in Garberville, KPFA in Berkeley, and several others originate weekly features pertaining to Indian issues.

Public stations such as these and others have provided opportunities in a variety of areas for many aspiring Native producers and broadcasters. Recounts E. B. Eiselein,

While at KUAT in Tucson, I conducted research using surveys, participant-obser-vation, focus groups, and formal interviews. In addition, I produced, directed, and hosted both radio and television programs. For example, on KUAT-AM, I was producing and hosting 6 to 10 five-minute interview programs each week and 2 half-hour call-in programs. These programs focused on topics such as Indian education, health care, religion, and urban living. One of the long-term things that I was involved with was the Papago Radio Project. After several years of discussing with Papago leaders the potential for radio to serve Tohono O'odham people, we were funded for a two-year project to train a group of Papagos in radio broadcasting. As part of their training, this group produced a regular Papago program for the station. We had hoped that this project would lead to the establishment of a radio station serving the reservation. Unfortunately it did not.[46]

Of course, not all public stations near Native populations direct service to this audience segment. Station KCWC, for example, whose signal covers the Wind River Reservation in Wyoming, does not schedule regular broad-casts for the local tribes (Arapahoo and Shoshone). Nevertheless, "while we don't broadcast programs exclusively targeting Indians on a consistent basis, a number of our programs do address Native problems."[47]

Inspired by the lack of broadcast service for their people, the council leaders of the Wind River Reservation tribes have approved the pursuit of their own broadcast license.

The preceding discussion seeks to highlight rather than detail the evolu-tion of Native programming in America. There is little formal documenta-tion available pertaining to Indigenous broadcasting or the impact of mainstream media on Indian life, especially prior to the advent of Native-owned and -operated stations in the 1970s. Since the development of a Native broadcast industry, a canon of literature devoted to it has been slow to evolve. Because of the dearth of information, a comprehensive history on this topic would be a formidable challenge. However, such a study would doubtlessly add to our understanding of the role of electronic media in minority cultures.

*Chapter Two*

# Arrow with Voices: Evolution of Native Stations

> There was no one to talk to except the invisible world, nothing to move
> me but the music on the radio.
>
> —Joy Harjo, Creek writer and poet

## ORIGIN AND PURPOSE OF NATIVE STATIONS

Hundreds of years of exploitation and oppression by non-Indians, mainly
whites, served as the primary impetus behind the establishment of Native-
controlled broadcast media. The ever shifting pendulum of government
Indian policy had the effect of emotionally and materially bankrupting the
country's Indigenous peoples. A trail of broken treaties as far back as
colonial times hastened the decline of Indian fortunes. Indian lands became
the target of land speculators, including George Washington, after the
colonies won their independence from Great Britain. Thus the die was cast
for the dissolution of hundreds of land treaties between Indians and whites
under the banner of Manifest Destiny.

The goverment policy toward Indians between 1828 and 1887 involved
removal and relocation. What this approach sought was the expulsion of
Native Americans from lands perceived as necessary for the continued
expansion of Anglo culture. In order to develop this agriculturally rich soil,
"Europeans feel that the solution is to remove the Indians from the land so
that the land can be 'used.'"[1]

The title is an elder's reference to a station's antennas.

The Indian Removal Act of 1830 forced Indians to move from parts of the Midwest to the western plains. "Originally this 'Indian Territory' included all of present-day Kansas, most of Oklahoma, and parts of Nebraska, Colorado, and Wyoming."[2] Eventually the size of this territory was reduced in order to accommodate white settlers in the region. Such reduction became a familiar theme as non-Indians ultimately extended their claims to the Pacific Ocean.

A shift in U.S. policy toward Indians, expressed by the Dawes Act, occurred between 1887 and 1928. The idea behind this legislation was to make farmers out of Native Americans by allotting them a piece of land (160 acres to families and 80 acres to single people) and forcing them to assimilate white agricultural techniques. This policy was perceived as a means of civilizing the "redskin." "Europeans strongly feel that land is to be used for farming and therefore Indians should be farmers. Thus we have an era in which Indian people are forced to become farmers and to adopt a European view of the nature of land."[3] The Dawes Act also resulted in Native Americans being forced out of communal land ownership situations, a change that was at the center of the plan that was designed ultimately to remove obstructions to the fuller development of Anglo interests.

The government's policy toward Natives embodied in the Dawes Act was superseded by yet another plan implemented between 1928 and 1945. The 1934 Indian Reorganization Act encouraged Native Americans to establish their own governments and communities. This policy brought about government-sanctioned tribal councils and tribal political organizations on many reservations, although there was resistance to this new policy in some areas.

After World War II, another swing in U.S. policy towards Indians was initiated. A government commission recommended full assimilation by Indians into mainstream culture. Once again, the motive behind this change arose from the ambitions of the dominant culture. "European-American interests see the economic potential in lands which are part of Indian reservations and thus begins the termination of reservations and Indian peoples."[4]

This policy was enacted until 1961, when yet another move in government Indian policy ended assimilation and led to the present era of Indian empowerment and self-determination. In the 1960s, Native Americans resoundingly rejected the paternal rule of the "Great White Father" in favor of playing a greater role in their own affairs and destiny. The Red Power movement was born against a backdrop of civil unrest stemming from a call by African Americans and other minorities for equal rights. This call was a primary catalyst. "Indian 'militants' follow the example of the Black Civil Rights Movement and begin to press their own claims for Indian civil rights."[5]

Wilma Mankiller, principle chief of the Cherokee nation, makes the following observation:

The torch of protest and change was grasped by Native Americans. The rage that helped to give a voice and spirit to other minority groups spread through Native people like a springtime prairie fire. And just as the tall grass thrives and new life bursts forth after the passage of those indispensible flames, we too were given a renewal of energy and purpose.[6]

Concerning this period of growing Indian activism, Native writer Vine Deloria, Jr. observed that "The middle ground of progressive ideology in Indian affairs was fast eroding and desperate confrontation was in the air."[7]

Out of this crusade for equal rights came the American Indian Movement (AIM). Established in the late 1960s, the movement "came into existence as a direct result of the termination and relocation programs that dumped thousands of bewildered Indians into cities."[8] AIM was founded by Clyde Bellecourt, Eddie Benton Banai, George Mitchell, and Dennis Banks, most of whom had earned high profiles as Indian activists. In so doing they and their followers had inspired the contempt and incurred the wrath of the FBI and other federal and state law enforcement agencies, which classified them as extremists.

The idea behind AIM was to "educate people on issues that affected their lives."[9] Its "warrior spirit had restored identity and pride to thousands of defeated people and inspired [them] to resurrect a dying language and culture."[10] "AIM created a feeling of solidarity among Indians."[11] AIM's primary function was to call attention to the human rights violations against Native Americans and to ensure that the American Indian culture would not be exterminated. "During the social upheavals of the late 1960's, this all-important credo—to help the people—was more relevant than ever. The struggles of Indian people were coming to the forefront of the nation's attention, and a resurgence of Indian cultural expression was a significant part of the fight."[12]

AIM's "warrior spirit" often brought it face to face with Anglo authorities and occasionally other Indian groups. Not all Native Americans were supporters of AIM's aggressive tactics and policies. Nonetheless, AIM did contribute significantly to a growing appreciation by Native Americans for the power of the media.

AIM's seizure of Wounded Knee, South Dakota, in 1972, and its use of the media to dramatize the situation, raised Native American awareness of the potency of television and radio. "In a lengthy standoff with the FBI that threatened to turn into a bloodbath, the Indians staged effective media presentations that again captured the attention of the nation."[13] The media (television in particular) were an integral part of AIM's strategy to expose to the world what it perceived to be gross injustices against its people. Broadcasting was a key player in launching its movement. "Clearly indebted to the examples established by the campus and Black militants who had preceded them, the red militants used media to maintain enthusiasm and popular support. . . . Events were staged as much for their media potential as for their significance to the issues."[14]

This development would subsequently contribute to the idea of Native-controlled and -operated broadcast stations. "AIM helped create the environment in which Native electronic media could happen. It brought about the reawakening that was necessary for this step to be possible,"[15] observes national AIM leader Vernon Bellecourt.

Says ICA's Ray Cook, "There's no doubt that AIM helped plant the seed and heighten Native appreciation of the power of the media, but it cannot be solely credited with making this happen. AIM really didn't prompt communities to organize to form media. This is something they did mostly on their own, often inspired by their own experiences with America's media fascination with Natives."[16]

Mark Tilsen, cofounder of KILI–FM, which stands a few miles north of Wounded Knee, agrees. "AIM certainly played a role, but I wouldn't want to give too much credit to the national leadership."[17]

The Chippewa novelist Gerald Vizenor perceives AIM as more of a public relations group than a mediator. "The American Indian Movement has raised good issues through the press, but it has seldom followed through to negotiate."[18]

Cook believes the 1934 Indian Reorganization Act began to stir interest among Indians about the potential use of electronic media, and Indian policy scholar Francis Prucha contends that the idea of using broadcasting may well have sprung from the act. "Indian communities were encouraged to re-establish tribal governments, which were able to take actions that before were generally impossible. So there was an organized government of sorts that could promote and support radio. All this came very shortly after the advances in radio broadcasting in the 1920's."[19]

From Chief Mankiller's perspective, the Economic Opportunity Act of 1965 helped set the stage for the creation of tribal licensed radio stations.

"This new law allowed Native American organizations and tribes to bypass the BIA [Bureau of Indian Affairs] while they planned, developed, and implemented their own social, educational, and economic initiatives. For some Native communities and reservations, it was the beginning of economic self-determination."[20]

Some four years after the implementation of the Economic Opportunity Act, Mankiller herself would be involved in an historic Indian action at Alcatraz, which in the eyes of many would be the catalyst for the creation of Native-controlled broadcast outlets in the United States. "The takeover of Alcatraz in 1969 is a significant event in the 'Red Power Movement.' The Indians take possession of the island in the name of all American Indians. They issue a proclamation reclaiming the island by right of discovery and offer the United States $24 in beads and trade cloth for it."[21]

This proclamation and dozens of other statements by those occupying the island were broadcast via Pacifica station KPFA–FM in Berkeley between November 1969 and June 1971. The station loaned the Indians on the island a Marti transmitter to send their message to the station, which then broadcast it live to listeners in the Bay Area. Radio Free Alcatraz, as it was called, focused on the impoverished state of Indian affairs, demanding that attention be paid to Indian health, education, and cultural issues.

From the perspective of those who occupied the small island, radio was the medium whereby the truth could be conveyed. It could leap barriers and roadblocks and reach the ears and hearts of the public. "This impressed Natives everywhere, and it definitely got people thinking about having their own broadcast facilities. Alcatraz was a turning point in Indian self-determination. It was the point of conception for Nationalist Native broadcasting, you might say."[22]

The construction of Native-owned radio stations began in 1971 at the height of the Indian rights movement. It was felt that these stations would further empower Native Americans in their quest for fair and just treatment. "As more and more Natives learned about the opportunity to have a voice of their own on their reservation, radio stations were built."[23]

The desire by Native Americans to control their own destiny, manage their own information, and preserve their culture fueled the development of Native-controlled broadcast stations. Many Native tribes ran the risk of becoming overassimilated into mainstream culture, thus losing touch with their own history and heritage, and Native radio was seen as a possible means for slowing and possibly reversing this trend. The force of the three uninvited guests (organized religion, white education, English-language media) was taking its toll. "There was a very real danger of loss of cultural identity due to the lack of exclusive Native electronic media."[24]

The presence of mainstream media in many Native communities has contributed to the erosion of traditional life. Observes Mark Trahant, journalist and member of the Shoshone-Bannock tribe, "Whether we like it or not, the youth of Indian country are bombarded by cultural influences—from television to telephone—that are bound to change tribal cultures."[25]

At greatest risk in Indian country is the Native tongue, and the fear is "that if the languages die the culture will slip away as well."[26] To Native researcher E. B. Eiselein, the loss of language would be devastating to Indians.

Language is an integral part of culture. It is more than just an expression of culture. Language is a way of seeing the world, of interpreting reality. As anthropologists discovered long ago, in order to begin to understand another culture, it is necessary to understand the language. Language is more than words. It is a way of ordering physical and social reality, of understanding the relationship between the material and the spiritual. Thus for young people to understand the culture of their grandparents, they must understand the language of their grandparents. The degree to which Indian peoples use English instead of their native language is an indication of the degree of assimilation they have to Anglo culture. Speaking English means interpreting the world through Anglo culture rather than through Indian culture. Speaking English is associated with the European religion. Speaking Indian is associated with traditional religion.[27]

Native radio was perceived not only as a way to help retain their language but as a method for communicating to Indians who spoke a Native language exclusively. Many older Indians use English as a second language, if they use it at all, and were unserved by Anglo broadcasting stations.

Native-operated stations were also seen as potential tools to help combat the negative images and false impressions of Indians so prevalent in mainstream society. Mainstream broadcasting has contributed to an uncomplimentary view of the American Indian. "In the general media Indians are either invisible or they are shown as a European stereotype of Plains Indians, mounted warriors with feathered headdresses living in the 19th century."[28]

There have been very few flattering images of Indians on network radio. Indians have traditionally been portrayed as murderous fiends or mindless servants. In his study of early radio programming, J. Fred MacDonald cites only a handful of shows that cast Indians in a positive light, among them *The Cisco Kid* and *Straight Arrow*. According to MacDonald, there was an attempt at the network level toward a more positive depiction of Indians in the 1940s, but it had little staying power, as evidenced by a character in the

1950 program *Western Caravan*, who comments that "The only good Indian is a dead Indian."[29] Perhaps the most famous Native American to American television viewers was the Lone Ranger's faithful companion, Tonto, who "cemented in the minds of the American public the cherished falsehood that all Indians were basically the same—friendly and stupid."[30]

According to broadcast historian Erik Barnouw, radio was actually used to debunk the fact that Indians were poorly treated in the United States. Part of the text of a broadcast by Radio Liberty on May 2, 1960, went as follows: "In point of fact young Indians go to school, college, and universities, and even the older generation has long ago 'buried the hatchet.' " Barnouw reveals that "the glowing account went on to tell of the Navajo tribe of Arizona acquiring a computer to aid in management" of its various business concerns. "The modern Indian 'wigwam,' said one of the voices, had modern furniture and television. The only problem of its occupant seemed to be that his image on the television set was not quite satisfactory."[31]

Hence, Indians were determined that their own radio stations would eliminate these stereotypes and get the facts straight. According to Rose W. Robinson of the National Congress of American Indians:

The general media never covered Indian affairs except when it was about crime, tragedy, or a stereotypical event or activity. They never had any interest in providing news of interest to Indian listeners or addressing misconceptions. Seeing the world through other eyes all the time can be frustrating and anger-provoking, because the Indian world is portrayed through the interpretations of those who always have a bias about that world—whether good or bad.[32]

When the first Native-operated stations went on the air in the early 1970s, it was with a feeling that at least at these broadcast operations Indigenous people would not be stereotyped, misrepresented, or denigrated. At these stations Native Americans would be provided with programming sensitive to their needs—programming celebrating the life and history of the country's first inhabitants. The first Native-licensed station represented a significant step in the Indian crusade to realign what continues to be skewed at the hands of the culture of the majority.

As to which Native station was first, there has been some debate, which usually leads to defining just what is meant by first. For instance, if by first we mean the first broadcast license awarded to a tribe, then WYRU–AM in Red Springs, North Carolina, may claim the title, since it began broadcasting in June 1970. However, it broadcast commercially, and its programming was intended for a general audience, which was viewed as the best way for it to attract potential advertisers.

KMDX-FM in Parker. Arizona claimed to be the first commercial Indian station, but ICA's records appear to refute this assertion, showing WYRU as the pioneer commercial Native radio station. KMDX went on the air in the mid-1970's, but was forced to pull the plug within a year because it was unable to successfully sell its airtime or collect payment on it once it had. However, both claims merit consideration when the distinction is made between that of a tribally-held license (WYRU) as opposed to one held by an individual Native American, which was the case with KMDX, whose owner was Gilbert Leivas. There are firsts and then there are firsts. Certainly, WYRU may claim to be the longest continuously operating commercial radio station licensed to a tribe. Admittedly, documentation is a bit vague on this point.

The first noncommercial, public station affiliated with a tribe was KYUK in Bethel, Alaska. According to information appearing in *Broadcasting and Cable Yearbook* (1992), it began broadcasts in May 1971 (FCC records show it was licensed a year later). Although it directed a substantial amount of programming to Indigenous listeners, the bulk of its schedule was aimed at a mixed audience.

Navajo station KTDB in Pine Hill, New Mexico, made its debut in April 1972 and fully directed its signal to Native listeners. Therefore it claims to be the country's premier Indian-only broadcast operation.

Says FCC mass media analyst Allen Myers, "According to my records, KTDB is the first Native-licensed public station. It would be difficult to ascertain if any tribe was issued a license before this date. I doubt it. Of course, keep in mind that stations conducted experimental on-air testing before being officially licensed. So this sometimes adds to the confusion as to who was on the air first."[33] Adding to the conundrum are those difficult to track stations that went on the air years back but went silent shortly after their launch date. KMDX is a good example, as is KIPC-FM (Pueblo Indian Radio in New Mexico, which sought to serve the state's 19 Pueblos. The station ceased broadcasting a few months after its debut, because it found it impossible to raise funds to continue operating. Internal conflict, related mostly to programming issues, also contributed to its untimely demise. As to whether individual Native Americans have held broadcast licenses prior to 1970, Myers says that it is quite possible but hard to determine based on past FCC record-keeping practices.

This issue aside, by the mid-1970s, a half dozen tribes were involved with the operation of radio stations. In less than half a decade, the nation's Indigenous peoples could claim possession of an evolving electronic media, whose progress would continue slowly but unabated into the 1990s.

Besides the landmark legislation that gave rise to government-funded public broadcasting, the initiation of the Minority Station Startup process by the National Telecommunications Information Agency (NTIA) and CPB in 1978 accelerated the development of Native broadcast media.

In the late 1970s and early 1980s, the climate for the growth of Indian electronic media continued to improve. "In the U.S., the general expansion of public radio into rural areas along with better organized and funded Native American organizations combined to construct early Native owned and operated broadcast facilities."[34]

While Native station numbers grew, their mission statements tended to resemble one another. Among the recurring themes was a determination to preserve Indian culture and language and a commitment to inform, educate, and entertain listeners in a manner that contributed to the enhancement of life in their signal areas.

## NATIVE-OPERATED TELEVISION

The lower cost required to put a radio station on the air in comparison to a television station has resulted in audio-oriented Native electronic media. In 1984, an effort was made by Sisseton Sioux Frank Blythe and the Commanche Wallace Coffey to put a ultrahigh frequency (UHF) television station on the air. After receiving a construction permit from the FCC, they made attempts to raise the money necessary to make the station a reality, but their attempts failed. Channel 45, as it was to have been called, would have been the first regular (commercial) television station licensed to Natives.

Although there is a strong desire to expand Native video service, movement in that direction has been extremely slow. "The bottom line is the prohibitive nature of the initial investment and then the cost of operation. It is still too expensive to own a TV station in most Native communities."[35]

Indians have engaged in television operation at one time or another over the last couple of decades, often to address specific social and political issues. Such was the case in this account in the National Federation of Community Broadcasters' (NFCB) *Community Radio News:*

In May, 1979, a confrontation between New York State and the Mohawk Nation at Akwesasne was brewing over the issues of jurisdiction. During this time a Traditional Longhouse Chief was arrested and taken into New York State custody by Tribal Police under orders of the State-sponsored Elective Tribal Council. Believing that more repression was coming their way, the Traditional Mohawks moved to occupy the Tribal Council building and Police headquarters and forced the disbanding of the Tribal Police system that was enforcing New York State laws on Mohawk territory.

After disbanding, New York State Police moved onto the territory to reestablish their jurisdiction. The Traditional people at Akwesasne were identified and targeted for reprisals by supporters of the state imposed Elective system and NYS Police. Fearing for their safety, the Traditional community moved to a defensible area of the territory and set up camp for the next two years as negotiations towards an end to the conflict took place and the matter [was] justly settled.

During the first week of the encampment, a little known event took place that would illustrate the potential that broadcast technology would have in helping Mohawk people talk to each other and to those who lived around the territory. The Traditional Mohawks felt that expressing their point of view on this matter could not be left totally to the media. They felt they needed to command, for a limited time, the medium that was to carry their message to the people.

They decided to broadcast statements by the Traditional Chiefs to their people via a crude television transmission on channel 6, a then unused frequency. A Mohawk electrical technician rigged a video signal generator to an in-line amplifier and a crudely designed antenna. The signal covered about a 6 mile radius and carried the Chiefs' messages for approximately one hour before the equipment burned out. Never before have the Mohawk had such an ability. This single deed, in the minds of the Mohawk, signaled the coming of a very calculated, radical change—Mohawk run broadcasting.[36]

This dramatic first experience with broadcasting ultimately led to the creation of the Native radio station CKON–FM, located on the U.S. and Canadian borders.

Several attempts have been made since the 1970s to get Native-operated television service onto some reservations. Unfortunately, with but a few exceptions, these efforts did not come to fruition. For example, plans for a tribal television station on Pine Ridge collapsed in the 1970s only to be resurrected in the 1980s and to meet with failure once again. The Nez Perce tribe in Idaho was hopeful of getting a low-power televison signal in the early 1980s, but owing to a series of frustrating setbacks, it never came about. In almost every instance, cost proved the primary stumbling block. "When you're starting radio, you're usually talking five figures. Television very often adds another digit."[37]

There exists only a handful of Native video signals. Among them is Navajo Nation TV 5 (NNTV–5), which re-airs PBS programming and originates five hours of Navajo-language features weekly over a local cable system. NNTV–5 was set to begin airing this programming over a UHF channel in the summer of 1994.

Native Americans employ cable channels in other parts of the country as well. On the Lower Brule Reservation in South Dakota, Native-language programming and features especially aimed at Native children are sent down Channel 20 of Sioux Satellite Cable five days a week. The programming is entirely local in nature and is produced by Bill Ziegler and a host of volunteers.

In North Carolina, the Eastern Band of Cherokee Indians uses a cable channel to telecast live their monthly tribal council meetings from the reservation. "The live coverage is widely watched and people call in during the meetings to voice their opinion through their Tribal Council representative. The meetings are recorded and are shown in the evenings for tribal members to watch and keep up to date on Tribal Council actions."[38]

Over-the-air television broadcasting is rarer, but it does exist. Perhaps the most prominent Native television operation is KYUK in Bethel, Alaska, which has been on the air since the early 1970s. While its board is comprised primarily of Indigenous people (Yup'ik Eskimos), its programming is geared for a mixed audience. KYUK–TV broadcasts in both English and Yup'ik and along with its AM radio counterpart covers an area about the size of Ohio.[39]

LPTV operations are springing up in and around various reservations. One example is Channel 56, which debuted despite the freeze imposed on the licensing of low-power television stations in the late 1980s. The station, also known affectionately as "Purple Cow" television, has been offering several hours of weekly programming to people in the Navajo nation who could not receive television programming without a costly satellite dish. The station's local programming is produced by students at the Rock Point Community School. (More detailed information on the preceding stations may be found in chapter 4.)

ICA is optimistic about continuing growth in the area of Indian-operated television. Many in the Indigenous community feel that expansion of video services tailored to their needs is crucial for all of the same reasons that inspired the creation and growth of Native-operated radio.

Says AIM spokesperson Carole Standing Elk, "There needs to be a broader effort to bring about more Native television. Things haven't been moving as fast as they should in this area. I hope it happens."[40]

## NATIVE STATION LICENSING

With but one exception, all Native broadcast facilities operate under the auspices of the FCC. Tribal governments or local school boards are the principal licensees. KILI in South Dakota is licensed to a corporation.

A number of Native Americans think that their stations should not come under the control of the federal government but that they should be viewed as sovereign entities under the tribes that operate them. Adhering to this principle of autonomy, CKON has its license issued by the Mohawk government. Despite the fact that its antenna and studios are on different sides of the border, "Neither the Canadian Radio and Television Commission (CRTC) or the Federal Communications Commission (FCC) license this station."[41]

ICA is in favor of similar licensing arrangements at other Native-operated stations. "Only one Indian Nation actually owns and regulates its airwaves. Some Native observers find it ironic that Indian communities in possession of such a powerful tool as radio would entrust its licensing and regulation to the U.S. Federal government."[42]

Sovereignty is a major issue for most Native Americans, and the idea of the federal government playing a key role in the regulation of Indian media is one that does not sit well with them. "Indian people must control their own destiny. This control is sometimes expressed in the word 'sovereignty,'"[43] observes E. B. Eiselein, who adds that gaining true autonomy in Indian country will require changes in the federal government's approach to Native affairs. "Implementation of sovereignty requires some changes in the Bureau of Indian Affairs (BIA). As long as the BIA continues as a paternalistic bureaucracy which dictates what Indian nations can and cannot do, there can be no sovereignty. The BIA must come to see itself as a consultant to Indian nations rather than as a parent caring for children."[44]

Because Native station signals often carry beyond Indian country, the FCC is disinclined to observe a hands-off policy towards them. "It is not the land that is at issue, but rather the air. It is the Commission's job to preserve spectrum integrity in this country. I don't see separate licensing happening,"[45] says the FCC's Allen Myers.

Despite this position by the federal government, Indigenous broadcasters appear committed to the ideal of sovereignty for their stations. Comments ICA's Ray Cook, "These signals belong to Indian territory and should not be subject to policies established by foreign governments."[46]

While ICA's secretary, Joseph Orozco, appreciates the wisdom in this view, he is dubious about Native station autonomy. "Even with sovereignty from the federal government, there will be a need to set regulation standards. Given the First Amendment problems most stations face with their tribes, boards, and councils, I would be wary about giving each tribe separate jurisdiction of its territorial airways. To act in a sovereign manner, I see the need to form a Native communication commission."[47]

## Chapter Three

# Abetting Silakkuagvik: Native Broadcast Funding

In the Sioux language, radio is described as words that fly through the air.
—Frank Blythe, executive director,
Native American Public Broadcasting Consortium

## FINDING SUPPORT

Support for Native-operated stations has come from a variety of sources, chief among them the Corporation for Public Broadcasting and the National Telecommunications Information Agency. While the former was instrumental in launching the Indigenous Communications Association—the first and only organization of Native American radio stations—NTIA breathed life into several Native broadcast projects through its Public Telecommunications Facilities Program (PTFP).

Although Native-controlled electronic media grew out of the Indian civil rights movement, whose principal goal was the cessation of centuries of government interference, manipulation, and exploitation, aspiring Indigenous broadcasters would find in this declared adversary of their people a major benefactor in their efforts to reach the airwaves.

### Corporation for Public Broadcasting

As a principal funder of public broadcast stations in the country, CPB has allocated millions of dollars to the operation of Native stations through

*Silakkuagvik* is Inupiat for "communicating through the air."

several minority broadcasting initiatives that date from the 1970s. Its expansion-grants programs have fostered the development of many Native stations, among them KILI, KMHA, and KNNB. The list of recipients of CPB subsidies has been formidable, although support for new Native stations dwindled somewhat in the 1980s as government outreach efforts were reduced.

Long apprehensive about their status in the CPB funding pecking order, Native Americans are also wary of the continuing debates on Capitol Hill regarding public broadcasting funding, which is under constant scrutiny by a Congress that is perennially in search of places to make spending cuts. During the Reagan and Bush administrations, funding for Native American programs decreased by 40 percent. The pie continued to shrink into the 1990s, causing rising anxiety levels among Native Americans.

CPB's funding mission includes allocating dollars for station operations in any part of the country without a public radio signal as well as support for minority-owned and -operated broadcast facilities. CPB grants have been used from the station-planning phase through the upgrading of operations once a station is on the air. With the acceptance of these subsidies, these stations become members, so to speak, of the CPB tribal confederacy, a fact that does not sit well with some indigenous broadcasters.

## National Telecommunications Information Agency

Mary Dinota, who served as NTIA/PTFP's special concerns officer responsible for encouraging minorities to utilize telecommunications facilities, credits assistance from this particular federal program with helping create Native electronic media.

Back in the 1970's and early 1980's, I attended a number of minority-related conferences, including those hosted by various Native organizations, and was able to encourage a number of the reservation leaders to construct public radio stations as well as other public telecommunications facilities (a low-power television station in Montana, a production facility for a Native-owned cable system in Alaska, and a cable system in North Carolina which reserved several channels for educational purposes). Very few "minority" public radio stations existed at the time Congress gave PTFP its mandate to increase participation of minorities and women in public telecommunications facilities. The PTFP commitment in those early days resulted in there being nearly a dozen new Native-controlled radio stations in some stage of planning, construction or broadcasting.[1]

The Public Telecommunications Facilities Program provides support for the acquisition of needed broadcast equipment, while the Corporation of Public Broadcasting makes funds available for station operations, programming, and training.

In 1993, PTFP made more tha $20 million available for television and radio technical upgrade and extension projects. Distant-learning projects received the bulk of the funds, while only two Native stations were awarded start-up grants. It was fervently hoped by members of the Native community that greater financial support would be forthcoming from PTFP/NTIA in the years to come.

## National Federation of Community Broadcasters

A strong alliance exists between Native stations and the NFCB, which has provided assistance to Indigenous broadcasters during the FCC licensing process and grant-proposal phase with both CPB's and NTIA's programs. "The NFCB staff has provided advice, consulting, and training services. We have embraced these stations as exemplifying community radio at its core—using telecommunications to provide information and entertainment focused on the needs of the local community,"[2] says the organization's president, Lynn Chadwick.

In its media brochure, NFCB describes itself as a "grassroots organization of non-commercial, educational, public radio stations distinguished by their community support, control, and programming." As members of NFCB, Native stations receive representation before key groups in Washington—Congress, CPB, FCC, NTIA, and other important sources of support.

NFCB also provides its member stations with other dispensations, among them: information and assistance (referral services) related to daily operational questions, FCC rules and regulations, management and organizational development, technical issues, and fund-raising sourcing.

NFCB's philosophy of local community control and "commitment to community access, especially for those normally excluded from the mass media: women, ethnic groups and people of color, the elderly and young people,"[3] make it particularly appealing to Native stations.

## Indigenous Communications Association

Meanwhile, ICA is to Native broadcasting what the National Association of Broadcasters (NAB) is to mainstream radio and television operators, although this is not a particularly accurate analogy. Founded in 1990, with the assistance of CPB's Minority Station Improvement Program (MSIP), and incorporated in 1991 by fifteen Native radio station managers, ICA's declared purpose "is to provide development, advocacy, and technical support to member stations."[4]

ICA's Ray Cook believes the creation of the organization was essential for the continued growth of Native broadcasting.

The very need for ICA intervention for Native radio indicates to the initiated that misconceptions and assumptions about Native America needed to be addressed. ICA, as a network of Native owned radio stations, who represent the Native communities that sustain them, can truthfully claim it is the only organization representing Native broadcasters. While other organizations, such as CPB, NPR, NFCB, APRN, NAPBC, NTIA, may service individual Native stations, they cannot make the representational claim. The governance of ICA by the Native station members gives it an insider's view of the day to day realities, desires, and capabilities of Native radio. Meeting the needs of Native stations to ensure their continued existence and growth is ICA's mandate. Whether it has to do with working to guarantee First Amendment rights for stations or assisting them in fund raising efforts and personnel training, ICA is there.[5]

According to ICA's membership brochure, the organization seeks to strengthen Native radio through the following:

- financial resource development and management
- advocacy and communications designed to promote station stability and growth
- station staff development and training
- international, national, and regional program production and dissemination
- enhancement of the impact of Native radio cross-cultural programming for expanding audiences worldwide

In its final interim report on its activities to CPB, ICA listed organizations it has worked with in the development of their training workshops, seminars, and meetings, which focus on rural Native concerns. Among the groups ICA has teamed with in efforts to enhance understanding of Native issues and needs are the Solidarity Foundation, the Native American Journalist's Association, the Indigenous Broadcast Center, the Smithsonian Institute's National Museum of the American Indian, the New York Times Corporation, Superior Radio Network, Monitor Radio, Community Media Services, NFCB, Radio Bilingue, Public Radio Forum, and NAPBC, to name a few.

The 1994 report summarized ICA's successes and enumerated its goals:

When ICA began full operation 2 years ago it had 15 member stations. Those are the stations which helped create ICA. At the time we knew of no start-up station projects. The Native stations in Alaska were solely dependent on the Alaskan Public Radio Network for their needs. Since then ICA has recruited 8 Alaskan Native owned stations, 2 other operating stations in the contiguous 48 states, and is advising 11 station start up projects. This brings ICA's membership up to 25 on-air stations and 11 start ups. ICA hopes to increase its station start up assistance by establishing resources specifically for that purpose. We want to go beyond a strictly advisory role. We want to create a relationship with our member stations that actively assists them in locating matching funds, quality technical and engineering talent, and in establishing a program of management training.[6]

ICA meets at the National Federation of Community Broadcasters' annual convention. It is at this gathering that Native broadcasters gather en masse to chart their future course. One of their goals is eventually to convene annually as an autonomous body. "As our association grows, this will not only be desirable but necessary,"[7] says Cook.

The following ICA manifesto stemmed from a meeting of the association's leaders during its inception stage:

People have a habit of identifying things in vague terms. For example, what is Native Radio or Indian Radio? People may be speaking to specific issues or certain situations, but their vague vocabulary is misleading.

When people talk about their personal Native radio station, they usually call it Native Radio. When people get together from two or more Native radio stations, they again call themselves Native Radio. The term Native Radio used by Natives from Native radio stations in this case is both a singular and plural identification. Both forms are correct considering the perspective from which these folk speak. However, when agencies like CPB talk about serving Native Radio they generally mean serving individual Native entities.

NAPBC claims to serve Native radio in a plural sense, but its efforts to serve other forms of electronic media dilute its radio participation. Even APRN [Alaska Public Radio Network] has said it serves Native Radio, but it primarily serves Native stations in Alaska. These three agencies serve individual Native stations. Yet no one could accurately say that they served Native Radio before the establishment of ICA. The association was born of the joining together of all Native stations, and it was this singualr event that makes ICA the representative agency of this unique medium.

Before the inception of ICA, Native Radio did not exist. There were Native O&O's, but they stood essentially alone. No agency represented them exclusively. CPB, NAPBC, APRN, NFCB, APR, NAJA, NPR, and other regional groups can claim that they offer services to individual Native stations, but ICA is Native Radio, by virtue of its governance structure, orientation of services, and vision.

ICA is what the name implies. We are *the* "Association" of Indigenous Communications. The word association is a plural term. Our governing members are individual Native stations. Our associate members include independent Native producers. Our affiliates include other Native organizations. The services we offer and the enterprises we establish, such as AIROS, make ICA the real "Native Radio Network." Such concepts did not exist nor were they made manifest until ICA was formed.

Other organizations, like CPB, can continue to serve individual Native stations. APRN can still serve the group of Native stations in Alaska. However, they can only honestly claim the limits of that reality. If these agencies deal with ICA to distribute their services to Native stations, then they can say in earnest that they serve Native Radio.[8]

### Indigenous Broadcast Center

The Indigenous Broadcast Center, a project of the Alaska Public Radio Network, is "the country's only national training center dedicated to increasing the participation and advancement of Native Americans in the public radio industry."[9] The purpose behind the center's existence is to make training available to Natives who work in public radio. IBC characterizes its mission as twofold: "to open up employment for Native Americans, a group that currently faces critically high levels of unemployment; and, to increase and enhance media coverage of issues affecting Native Americans."[10]

IBC conducts workshops in programming, engineering, and announcing for Native broadcasters and producers at its headquarters in Anchorage, and it offers on-site training at Native-operated stations as well.

### Native American Public Broadcasting Consortium

While NAPBC in Lincoln, Nebraska, is also involved in the training of Indians who work at public stations and those who seek broadcast employment, its reputation comes from its being the nation's foremost archive for Native programming. Since 1977, "NAPBC has accepted the responsibility for being the authoritative national resource for authentic, culturally educational and entertaining programming by and about Native Americans. Public broadcasters and educators from across the country look to NAPBC to provide an unparalleled selection of programs to intrigue, inform, and enlighten."[11]

NAPBC has been a central player in the development of Native telecommunication services as well. In collaboration with CPB and ICA, it has worked to bring about the existence of the first Native satellite radio network. It has also been involved in a project designed to connect the nation's twenty-seven American Indian colleges through the use of telecommunications technology.

One of NAPBC's principal functions is to offer consulting for Native American public television productions and to provide co-production development and national distribution. It has been under the direction of Frank Blythe since its inception.

## National Association of Broadcasters

The NAB, the nation's largest broadcast support group, has had little interest and involvement in Native radio, due principally to the association's commercial orientation. However, its vice president of human resource development, Dwight M. Ellis, claims that the association is sensitive to the needs of all minority broadcasters.

In its mission to serve the business needs and responsibilities to the American public, the NAB has demonstrated since the early 1970's a commitment to assisting the growth of employment and station ownership for minorities in the industry. From the institution of the industry's first broadcast industry employment clearinghouse (currently in operation within the Department of Human Resources Development) to its leadership in fostering the first industry-sponsored entity providing funding assistance for the purchase of radio and television stations by minorities, the NAB has been a vanguard for minority progress in broadcasting. Nevertheless, more must be done to encourage and advance Native American broadcasting.[12]

During his tenure as senior vice president of radio for the NAB, Lynn Christian found few initiatives directed toward Native stations. "There just wasn't much being done. Of course, very little was known about these stations. There was some sense that they were out there, but that was about it."[13]

## Funding Sources

The money to put Native signals on the air and keep them there comes from a mix of sources. Most of them are governmental (either federal or tribal), since all but a handful of Indian-operated stations are public and noncommercial.

There are other sources. One station receives partial funding from a Catholic mission, while "agressive fund raising is the key to survival for many stations. KMHA in New Town, North Dakota, raises money from a bingo operation and by selling advertising in a community newspaper it operates."[14]

Other unique approaches are used to fill station operation coffers. Everything from car washes to bean suppers are employed to raise crucial funds.

Instead of depending on traditional pledge weeks at KYUK, a live open house, on-the-air combination potluck supper, dance, auction, and local talent show is held on two consecutive nights and is simulcast on both KYUK AM and TV. The result is much like a neighborhood block party with contributions of nearly ten dollars for every man, woman, and child in the town of Bethel. During the remainder of the year, additional fundraising for KYUK depends largely on weekly bingo games and raffles.[15]

Many other Native stations take innovative approaches to fund raising. For instance, KABR in New Mexico broadcasts a live softball tournament; money is generated through entry fees and the sale of concessions at the ballpark. Meanwhile, KCIE, another New Mexico Native station, raises funds by holding a Fourth of July beach party, replete with sand that is hauled by truck to the site of the event.

Major corporations provide grants for certain Native broadcasting efforts. For example, APRN's Indigenous Broadcast Center receives funding from the M. J. Murdock Charitable Trust and General Mills, as well as NEA's Challenge Grant Program and CPB. The latter's Minority Station Improvement Program provided more than $300,000 in start-up funds to help create the center.

As previously mentioned, CPB grants also contribute significantly to the operation of ICA. In addition they benefit NAPBC, which finds further support from the Nebraska Educational TV Network, its public broadcast station members, and Native American and educational group members who utilize the consortium's various services. NAPBC also receives grants from other organizations, foundations, and corporations.

## Funding Issues

Lack of funding is the biggest problem confronting Native stations. "Things are drying up on the federal level, and they have always been pretty arid on the home front,"[16] observes Joe Orozco.

For the past several years, the major concern at CPB has been congressional cutbacks of its funding. These have sent shock waves throughout the public broadcasting community and caused Native broadcasters to wonder what these actions bode for them.

"Whatever happens, you can bet Native broadcasters will be on the short end of the stick. We're already standing at the far end of the line when it comes to federal funding of our medium. Getting up is one thing, but staying up is another. The way things are going, neither may be possible in the future,"[17] says Orozco.

The withering of federal funding is a concern for those Native stations that qualify for CPB funding. However, not all stations are eligible for CPB support, because CPB requires that stations generate a specified level of local funding before they qualify for assistance.

The formula used by the Corporation of Public Broadcasting to award grants tends to disadvantage Native stations because it matches local funds. In poor, rural communities where there is a minimal cash economy, such a system tends to disqualify Native stations from receiving any federal funds. Nearly half of the noncommercial Native stations receive no CPB funding. Those that are federally funded, especially outside Alaska, receive substantially smaller grants than the average for all public stations.[18]

For those stations unable to qualify for federal subsidies, the challenge of remaining afloat is often compounded. The lack of a viable local economy in most Native signal areas makes the job of meeting operational expenses difficult if not impossible. Traditional fund-raising techniques found at non-Indian public stations seldom are effective, a situation that has led to discussions focusing on other ways to keep Native stations on the air.

A 1987 report prepared by Nan Rubin and the NAPBC for presentation to CPB outlined the reasons why so many Native stations lack an ability to generate local funding support. Its conclusions are relevant today. The report stated as follows:

1. Most of the stations now rely on a single source for the majority of their operating funds: the tribal government, the tribal business council, or the tribal school board. In all cases, the source of funding for these bodies is federally-based. With recent major cutbacks in funding for Native American programs, these sources of funds are being withdrawn from the radio stations to be used for other, more pressing reservation needs. The stations are thus threatened with losing up to 95% of their operating funds within a short period of time, with little experience, assistance or opportunity to find replacement support within the short timeframe. Also those stations which are CPB qualified are at the mini-mally-qualified level, and even a slight decrease in funding could jeopardize this standing.

2. Because these stations are all in rural areas with sparse populations, even the stations which serve large geographic regions have an extremely small audience base to draw on for listener support. KILI, with 100,000 watts reaching most of southern South Dakota, has less than 40,000 people within its signal area; KNNB, serving the White Mt. Reservation in Arizona with 5 translators, reaches 15,000 potential listeners. The reservation populations are poor, with unemployment rates as high as 85%. By and large, they listen to their stations and rely on them, but they simply do not have the means to adequately fund station operations through direct donations.

3. Most of these reservations have few business enterprises. Off-reservation commercial activities are widely scattered and suffering greatly from the crisis in the farm and construction economies. Thus, underwriting support is not a major option for developing substantial, reliable station income.

4. In those states which provide support for public broadcasting, these stations operate outside that system. Because they are not part of a university-based or fine-arts state wide network, they are not eligible to receive state funds allocated to support these type stations. In some regions, the reservation stations have built their own translator networks and are seen by the state-funded broadcasters as direct competition.[19]

The leadership of ICA is researching new methods for generating funding, but a strategy has yet to be fully developed. "The business of Native broadcasting needs to change. That's the bottom line. The conventional nonprofit model doesn't work. We're always embroiled in a battle for federal support, or trying to raise funds where no funds exist. We'll need to form a network of some sort that provides an economic base. We cannot operate as individual stations," [20] says Joe Orozco.

Ray Cook agrees with his colleague that the old approach to funding is not relevant to Native stations. "We've been employing the public radio model, and it just doesn't work in most of Indian country. The majority of public stations are in areas where donation drives have a chance, and their listeners are often upscale to begin with, which means underwriter interest too. We're in a very different situation, so we've got to go in another direction."[21]

Similar conclusions have been reached by other members of the Native community. Says E. B. Eiselein, "If the stations are serving poor people on the reservations, then they are serving the people least able to afford to contribute."[22]

In 1994 a project was initiated by ICA and funded in part by the CPB Development Fund that seeks to develop a comprehensive plan for raising funds in the Native radio environment. The project is dubbed For Our

Benefit, which is derived from the Mohawk phrase "that which is for our benefit"—(*Onkwaia Take Ha'tshera*).

The plan calls for special workshops for Native stations, says Cook.

By identifying the fund raising approaches used by member stations, we plan to facilitate workshops that will share strategies and teach stations how to maximize funding opportunities. These workshops will rely on the experience of our membership. This activity may be the first time any station has had an opportunity or the resources to share resources. A secondary use of this project is the accumulation of information that can be used to conduct a nationwide strategy. With this information in hand we can approach the agencies doing business in our territories and create a rationale to channel more funding from their communications budgets into broadcasting.[23]

To compound financial matters even further, precious money is commonly spent inappropriately and with unfortunate results. Veteran Native broadcaster Delfred Smith says this misuse of funds has kept some stations off the air:

During my two decades in public radio, I've heard of many Native radio stations about to be launched, but for reasons usually related to bad judgement—due mostly to a lack of expertise and knowledge on the part of individuals involved with these startups—these stations never happened. Thousands of dollars are often spent needlessly by small public radio stations, which can ill-afford to do this. I recall one Indian station paid a consultancy firm ten thousand dollars to do a feasibility study to upgrade their 10 watt station to 100 watts. In my opinion, this was a totally unnecessary thing to do. 100 watts wasn't going to significantly change their signal area, and for the same money they could have upgraded their power much more meaningfully, to say 1,000 watts. I'm sure that many other Native American stations, both radio and TV, spent money like this. This happens because folks at these stations just don't know better, and then they get burned and the station suffers. There are a lot of good intentions out there, but a lot of empty frequencies as the result of misdirected actions.[24]

The annual operating budgets for Native stations are relatively low compared to mainstream stations. While Alaskan station budgets are the most substantial ($700,000 at KBRW), several Native stations in the continental U.S. operate with less than the annual income of most urban professionals. According to statistics gathered by Bruce Smith and Jerry Brigham, in the early 1990s New Mexico stations KTDB and KABR operated with yearly budgets under $50,000.[25]

The following is excerpted from the keynote speech to ICA members by Native media expert and pioneer Charles Trimble at the NFCB Conference in 1994. Trimble illuminates the issue of fund raising:

When your radio stations are trying to raise funds on the reservations you must keep in mind that you are not working in a normal economy. I'm not just talking about the distressed economic condition of much of our Indian communities. You are working in an entitlement syndrome resulting from years of forced dependency on the federal government. Much more can be said about this, about how national Indian policy called for the systematic alienation of our economic base as a means of removing tribes from their homelands and fulfilling their philosophy of manifest destiny. But the net effect has been our deplorable condition of economic dependency.

In that entitlement syndrome, our people sometimes tend to believe that all funding and all services are entitlements from the federal government, including radio service. When I served on the board of the American Indian National Bank, which was capitalized by the investment of precious tribal funds and had no federal funds at all, many Indians saw it as just another federal source of funds. Our loan portfolio suffered because some of our people saw the loans from that bank as federal grants.

Your work is to convince the tribal publics that the station is theirs, and it is their responsibility to contribute their share to its continued operations.

You must also understand that reservation economies and the peripheral economies that feed off the reservations are better sources of funds than may be thought. The *Lakota Times* newspaper, now *Indian Country Today*, was started in the poorest single county in the U.S. That newspaper's publisher, Tim Giago, will take his place in Indian history, not as a journalist, but as an entrepreneur, who effectively commercialized the press. What he saw in that impoverished market was the great amount of money that comes from federal transfer payments. He has been very creative in getting at those federal transfer payments. If you analyze the advertising in his paper, you will see that a majority of the ads are for Indian schools and functions paid for by federal and tribal governments.

Federal transfer payments are an integral part of the economy of the reservations. You should be creative as well in finding ways to tap those public resources, being careful that even though you might be supported indirectly by public funds, you are not controlled by the politics of public officials. Also, tribal discretionary income is increasing with the phenomenal growth of Indian gaming. Much of that income must by law be spent on tribal public resources, such as education, economic development, and infrastructure. And generally, given the controversy surrounding Indian gaming, they need noble causes to offset any adverse publicity. Yours is a noble cause. You must convince yourselves, your community, and your tribal governments that you are an integral part of the community and the democracy of the Tribe.[26]

## COMMERCIAL NATIVE STATIONS

Of the more than two dozen Native-owned and -operated stations in the United States, only four are commercially licensed. As such they have little to do with the funding sources so vital to the existence of their broadcast brethren.

The public broadcasting initiatives of the 1970s and 1980s (which made funds widely available for Native radio projects), coupled with the lack of a sufficient economic base for advertiser-supported stations in most Native communities, resulted in a predominantly noncommercial medium.

Commercial Native-licensed stations are first and foremost bottom-line oriented. The idea is to make a profit with these stations. Some do, while others do not.

The climate for Native involvement in commercial broadcasting appears to be improving as the consequence of several economic factors, not the least of which is the rapid growth of the Native gaming industry, which may look to radio and television as possible investment sources for its vast profits. However, not everybody is confident that this new found affluence will benefit Native broadcasters. Meanwhile, growth in the number of commercial Native stations specifically targeting the Indigenous community may remain slow because of the negative perception of this market by many advertisers.

According to E. B. Eiselein:

For a commercial Indian radio station to be successful, advertisers must be convinced that the Indian market is a market which they want to reach. The difficulty in finding advertising for commercial Indian radio often lies in the stereotypes which some businesses, particularly national advertisers, have about the affluence, or rather lack of affluence, among Indian peoples.[27]

## WYRU–AM

The first commercial Native-licensed station was WYRU–AM. Located in Red Springs, North Carolina, it is licensed to the Lumbee tribe. Despite its affiliation, WYRU's programming is directed to a non-Indian audience, which is considered more economically viable by the station's management. Its programming rationale is predicated on the following marketing data, which are conveyed in its station profile:

Red Springs is a combined industrial/agricultural community, located in the center of a populous triangle whose points are Fayetteville, Lumberton, and Laurinburg. WYRU is the only radio station inside this triangle, serving it from within and providing exclusive local news and informational programming. Nearby towns without radio stations of their own include Hope Mills, Maxton, Pembroke, Parkton, Lumber Bridge, and Shannon. These towns tune the station for their local news coverage. The area is the home of several plants that manufacture textile[s], fertilizer, and metal. The new Campbell Soup plant is here as well. Red Springs is surrounded by prosperous farmland. Tobacco is the principal crop, followed by soybean, corn, and cotton. By estimates of the North Carolina Council of Governments, the population with WYRU's signal is well in excess of 350,000.[28]

Gospel music (southern and black) comprises the bulk of the station's programming—from 5:45 A.M. until 3:00 P.M. The balance of the station's music programming consists of contemporary rhythm and blues. The station allocates airtime for farm news, weathercasts, community bulletin board information, and coverage of local college and high school sports and stock car racing.

Saturday is set aside for programming to Lumbee tribe members. "We air a mix of features that have relevance to our area's Native population, but we're primarily a mainstream operation. We're in the business to make money, which makes it possible to offer programming to the Lumbee people,"[29] says the station's program director, Al Stone.

According to the station, it has experimented with many different formats (country and western and big band music among them) since its first broadcast in June 1970, but it has always geared itself toward programming perceived as marketable to advertisers. The station's competition consists of a couple of area newspapers, and its signal is one of the area's most powerful—5,000 watts at 1160 kilohertz. Comments Stone, "We really blast a signal over Robeson, Hoke, Scotland, and Moore counties, and that makes us attractive to advertisers."[30]

The second commercial station licensed to Native Americans has not faired as well.

## WASG–AM

After broadcasting for nearly a dozen years, WASG–AM signed off the air in September 1993. Licensed to Poarch Creek Enterprises, the station found itself unable to support its operations and make a profit. Observes the station's co-owner Dale Gehman:

It was a combination of things that made us go dark—competition, the general status of AM broadcasting, but foremost I think was the attitude toward us in the community. We encountered problems with the fact that we were Native Americans trying to do business in the Anglo community. It was believed that the station was already supported by the government, so why did it need advertising revenue? When the station was turned over to the direct control of the tribe to see if it could make a go of things, there was a great deal of animosity from the white community. It seemed to confirm their suspicions. This only deepened the negative view of the station by the business community.[31]

During its years of operation WASG offered a full-service format that included a mix of music (gospel, country, adult contemporary) and news and information. In an attempt to be more marketable, it upgraded its signal to stereo and featured high quality, CD sound. "We had state-of-the-art studios and a very clean signal. We put a lot of money into the operation and felt we were really serving the community, so it's kind of disheartening to have what happened happen,"[32] says Gehman.

Although primarily targeting a mainstream audience, WASG did air weekly programs for its Indian constituency. "We devoted several hours of programs to Natives and broadcast tribal powwows as well, so we were comprehensively serving all the listeners within our service contours,"[33] Gehman adds.

The operators of the defunct station would like to see it back on the air but are not confident that this will happen. "Maybe things will change so that we can get the signal up and out again. I don't know whether the environment here will ever make us a viable enterprise. We've tried and would probably try again if it made good business sense to do so,"[34] observes Gehman.

WASG is probably the first and only tribally licensed commercial station to cease broadcasting. Allen Myers of the FCC says, "The only way to confirm this would be to scour the commission's station license files, and given the disposition of the archives (noncomputerized), this would amount to a pretty fair undertaking."[35]

## KTNN-AM

In 1986 the Navajo nation in Arizona put its 50,000-watt powerhouse, KTNN-AM, on the air. This event came at the end of a lengthy period of research on the viability of a commercial station operation. Jay Williams, Jr., and Joseph H. Helfgot of Massachusetts-based Broadcasting Unlimited were contracted to prepare a market study. Their findings supported the creation of an advertiser supported station. Based on the following reasons in the report, the Navajo Nation ventured into the field of commercial broadcasting.

1. Navajos account for a major proportion of retail sales. Retailers are aware of this and so are media buyers. Navajos shop more, spend more money, and travel further to make purchases.

2. Navajos drive a remarkable amount. Therefore, they spend more time listening to radio in their cars.

3. Navajos are predisposed to AM radio due to their more working class lifestyle.

4. If KTNN–AM can become the Navajo station in the FCTA, [Four Corners Trading Area], it can attract national and regional advertiser buys.

5. Navajos represent the largest proportion of young people entering the labor force. Among the counties with the largest proportion of young people, we also find the largest proportion of Navajos.

6. There is evidence of advertiser dissatisfaction with the current media for reaching Navajos while these same advertisers are increasingly attuned to the importance of Navajos as consumers.

7. Radio stations must develop a market story to be successful. The best market stories are those which are fine-tuned to the specific needs of a local market. The station which is community minded and is identifiable with a specific locality does best. Although the Navajo Nation is geographically dispersed over a wide land area, its fierce independence and general separation in distance and culture permit us to view it as a tightly knit community. If radio works best locally, it is difficult to imagine a more locally oriented community, not based on territory but principally on racial identity.

8. The population of Navajos in the FCTA is larger than other groups, while the competition among stations serving them is less.[36]

The report recommended that the new station offer a country music format based on the following assertions:

Because of the lack of Arbitron data for listening habits on the Reservation, our only valid empirical data on the format preferences of the Navajos comes from a marketing study in Gallup. Using an in-person/recall technique, stations offering rock music, on both AM and FM, did best followed by country and Navajo-language programming. This study was supported by our own in-person observations of Navajo listening habits both on and off the Reservation, with perhaps a slightly higher preference for country music. Because of the lack of data, important questions arise as to radio listening preferences through the Reservation. For example, what are the differences in listener preferences by demographics, especially considering the differences in format appeals among non-Navajos and the fact that some younger Navajos are bilingual? What are the differences in listening preferences among Navajos in the highly populated eastern edge of the Reservation who may be more assimilated with the Anglos from those in the interior of the Reservation? Yet, although a study of Navajo listening preferences would be ideal, certain assumptions can be made and a reasonably viable format can be recommended.

Navajos do show a preference for both country and rock music, and these formats are not incompatible. Based on observations of larger market listening preferences which historically trend more quickly than smaller, more rural markets, a country-oriented format would have more long term potential. Rock music, particularly utilizing artists with some country or cross-over origins, can be added to the country music base to add to the format's appeal, especially among younger listeners. In addition, some traditional "oldies" by rock artists such as Elvis Presley and Marty Robbins, who have country appeal, can be mixed in. This format would appeal best to known preferences of the Navajos, the long term potential preferences of AM listeners, and reflect the rural character of the station's coverage area.[37]

Local news and informational programming were suggested as a prime ingredient of KTNN's air product:

A frequently mentioned key to the success of any radio station is its ability to appeal to the local community. In this case, the local community is the Navajo Indian, regardless of location. All nonmusic programming should be directed at getting and keeping this listener, regardless of geographic location, by airing items of common interest. News programming, for example, should be concentrated in the morning hours (5–9AM), noon, and more briefly in the afternoon hours (4–6PM) based on times traditional listeners prefer to hear the news according to studies by the Associated Press and others. Such news programming should concentrate on events and stories that either affect the lives of or are of interest to Navajos on and off the Reservation. Events in the principal FCTA cities and towns should also be covered if they fit [those] criteria. This requires a network of correspondents reporting to the station to cover geographical areas served by KTNN. Other, less news-oriented events can be covered "topically" as part of the regular programming.[38]

The study addressed the language question and recommended that Enlish rather than Navajo be used as the primary tongue for the following reasons:

Advertisers interviewed believe the two languages reach two different types of Navajos; thus both languages should be used on the station to guarantee that KTNN has the potential of delivering both audience groups. In the absence of a listener survey on the reservation, but on the basis of a few in-person interviews, observations, and experience in other markets, Navajo-language programming,

**Figure 3.1**
**KTNN Promotional Sticker**

including music and news, might be broadcast from 5–6:30 AM and again from noon–3PM. English-language Navajo programming could be aired at other times. Weekends could be mixed, with more traditional Navajo-language programming principally broadcast in the mornings. Adjustments in actual English versus Navajo-language programming could be made based on listener response and advertiser contact.[39]

The report concluded that the lack of reliable listening data for KTNN's projected listening area pointed to the need for an in-depth study that would "pinpoint music preferences, language preferences, format viability by demographic, geographic differences, news orientation, and other information."[40] Since debuting, KTNN ("The Voice of the Navajo Nation") has conducted audience research to assist in its programming efforts, but the recommendations of the 1986 market study have remained essentially in place.

Both the English and Navajo languages are used, and music on KTNN is geared toward country and western. However, Native American music of both a traditional and contemporary variety is aired.

The station is heard throughout the Southwest (at night the station reaches as far as California, Oregon, and Idaho) and is among the most popular and profitable Native stations in the country, with many fans in other tribes, as well as a substantial number of non-Indian listeners.

The average price charged to advertisers for a sixty-second commercial is $20.00, and since the station is a Navajo Nation Enterprise, services are not subject to gross receipts sales tax.

KTNN is an NBC and Associated Press affiliate and has national sales representation. Among its most salient commercial ventures are its remote broadcasts from fairs, rodeos, businesses, sporting events, and public forums. Advertisers pay upwards of $1,800 to sponsor these highly regarded on-site broadcasts.

KTNN has been a success story from its inception, says its first general manager, Delfred Smith. "We were very solid from the start. Our collected revenues surpassed our payables, and with our disciplined news staff we became the number one news gathering station in the southwest, garnering 10 'Story of the Month' awards from the wire services. KTNN also gained national attention when it received NAB's 'Crystal Award' for outstanding public service."[41]

## K-TWINS

Oregon stations KTWI, KTWS, and KWSO are licensed to the Confederated Tribes of the Warm Springs Reservation. All of the stations are FM, and two are commercial—KTWI and KTWS.

In 1986 the tribes were licensed to operate KTWI (formerly KWSI) and noncommercial KWSO. Both stations were located on the reservation at Kahneeta. In December 1990 the tribes began operating a third station, their second to be commercially licensed. This station, KTWS, beamed its signals from Bend, Oregon, some seventy miles off the reservation.

The tribes combined their commercial FM signals in January 1991 to create K-TWINS. As such, the station's simulcast classic rock format covers a quarter of a million square miles and constitutes the state's superstation.

Behind this consolidation move was a desire to make KTWI more financially viable, as it was finding it difficult to "play" to the reservation. "There just wasn't enough accessible revenue in that market, so merging the two stations physically and image-wise was a good strategy that paid-off,"[42] says K-TWINS general manager John Stolz.

Marketed as "The Twins," the stations essentially operated as one, while employing the slogan "Two dial positions, two transmitters, and TWICE the music." The idea worked, and within six months K-TWINS became the most listened-to station(s) in central Oregon.

The revenues for 1991 surpassed all projections, and in 1992 K-TWINS established itself as the area's top-billing radio station. This was accomplished despite formidable competition in a part of the country considered to be overpopulated with broadcast outlets.

In 1994 the tribe planned to split the signals in order to get a larger share of the market revenue, offering classic rock music on one and an adult contemporary music on the other.

While KTWI operates with 100,000 watts, KTWS generates 12,800 watts. Neither specifically directs programming to Indians, but both claim a large number of Native listeners. K-TWINS spot rates are among the highest in central Oregon, and national advertising clients are numerous. The station is handled by one of the country's most prominent rep firms, McGavern Guild, which is an indication of its commercial viability.

## Cook Inlet Communications

In the early 1970s the Alaska Land Reclamation Act (which resulted in 100,000 Native Americans receiving nearly 44 million acres of land and a vast sum of money—$1 billion—in compensation for lands taken by white settlers) gave rise to a successful broadcast group known as Cook Inlet Communications. The company, part of the Cook Inlet Regional Corporation, owns several large-market radio and television stations, which broadcast to mainstream audiences in the continental United States.

Part of Cook Inlet's business strategy has been to take advantage of the government's tax certificate program for minority owners in its acquisition of television stations in New Haven, Connecticut, and Nashville, Tennessee. In 1993 the broadcast group expressed concern to the FCC about what it perceived as the fraudulent exploitation of minority certificates by "sham" companies, which set up operations by employing a token minority to create the impression of eligibility for minorities. Cook Inlet claims this practice is widespread and ultimately detrimental to the spirit and objective of the program.

As investors, the 6,700 Native Americans of the Cook Inlet Region share in the profits of the broadcast group, which foresees expanding its station portfolio.

## Passamaquoddy Broadcasting Incorporated

In December 1984 the Passamaquoddy tribe assumed the ownership of two commercial radio stations in Rockland, Maine—WRKD and WMCM. The tribe purchased the broadcast outlets as a revenue-producing venture. A half dozen years later, the tribe sold the stations for a profit, but it retained the real estate that housed the facilities. It left the business of broadcasting to become involved in a host of other investment ventures. There are no future plans by the tribe to become reinvolved with broadcast properties.

## NATIVE BROADCASTERS AND THE MAINSTREAMERS

There are ambivalent feelings concerning mainstream broadcasters. While some Native broadcasters perceive them in a fairly positive light, others are wary of them. To many aspiring Indian broadcasters, Anglo station personnel serve as role models, notes KGHR's general manager, Stu Schader:

In my opinion Native Americans perceive other broadcasters (Anglo) on the basis of performance and not race, creed, color, ethnicity, or cultural background. There is a bonding of Native Americans and Anglos through the medium of radio broadcasting. The students at KGHR's broadcast training facility see commercial radio announcers as their peers and role models because of their similar interests in the business. The same can be said of the Native American volunteers at the station. In the community of Tuba City there are primarily Anglo doctors at the Indian Health Services. Recently there was an outbreak of the haunta virus, and there was a need for the community to be aware of the situation. Native Americans, Anglos, and KGHR worked together to answer questions and work cooperatively to help the community. I envision the radio community working towards facilitating the needs of the Native Americans.[43]

Fellow Native station manager Barbara Maria says that a spirit of cooperation and mututal respect exists between Anglo and Native stations.

In general, Anglo stations pretty much stay within their own territories, since they target another type of audience. Sometimes we ask for help on something or other. For example, we go to the local mainstreamer to get information about weather conditions. We don't have equipment here at KTDB to monitor the weather in our signal area. So that alone establishes a connection between us. We help them, and in return they help us.[44]

It is when Native stations try to segregate themselves from the mainstream that tensions arise, contends KSHI's Duane Chimoni.

I believe, at least in our case, that the community has accepted mainstream broadcasting. To most listeners, broadcasters are broadcasters regardless of ethnicity. When we put restrictions upon ourselves and our perceptions of one another, that's when the conflict begins. Because so much acculturation has occurred within these past years, Native cultures have assimilated the "mainstream" of society, although "die-hard" seekers of their Native cultures will tell you differently.[45]

Although there have been few, if any, actual confrontations between Anglo and Native stations, the history of suspicion and distrust between the two cultures has increased the possibility. In fact, it was this distrust that contributed to the creation of Native station KINI, says its founder, Joseph Gill, "The Lakota people of Rosebud perceived the mainstream commercial media as basically antagonistic to and destructive of their values, and it was this that encouraged them to seek their own station."[46]

This distrust has been a widespread rather than an isolated phenomenon, says Native broadcast scholar and public station manager Bruce Smith.

Mainstream broadcast media have often been perceived as negative forces in Native communities. Broadcasting bombards Native communities with the sights and sounds of western culture, overwhelming Native languages and traditions. For example, Inuit [Eskimo] people of the North once feared that the introduction of television would further marginalize, rather than modernize, their people. One linguist, fearful of the impact of television, went so far as to call it a "cultural nerve gas."[47]

Distrust of mainstream broadcasters is something that has existed for a long time and will be around for a while longer, believes KSKO's former general manager, Susan Braine.

Overall, Native broadcasters tend to ignore Anglo broadcasters. Unless individual Anglo broadcasters express a genuine and sincere interest in reporting honestly— even Native broadcasters would rather represent Natives themselves. There is a question of trust between the two groups. This gap will take a long, long time to close, if it ever does.[48]

Fellow Alaska broadcaster Bob Sommer of station KIYU concurs with Braine, adding,

I think Native broadcasters look at the Anglo stations with a wary eye. They see them as generally not caring about what happens to Natives. For example, a Native community has a critical emergency with their sewer system for a period of a month before it's fixed. It would never even get on the Anglo newscasts until midway through the crisis, and then it would be given minor attention and airtime. If that same thing happened in the Anglo community, the mainstreamers would be on it every day. Right or wrong, this is how it is perceived.[49]

Resentment exists in the Native broadcasting community concerning the lack of employment opportunities for their people at mainstream stations. Anglo stations perceive Native on-air skills as largely inadequate to the challenge, contends E. B. Eiselein:

Anglo stations have traditionally discriminated against Native Americans, particularly in the area of on-air jobs. Since many reservation Indians have a distinctive accent, many station managers don't like to use Indians on the air. There have been occasions when program materials featuring Indian voices were even submitted to NPR for system-wide distribution, and these programs were rejected because the Indian accent was judged "monotone" and not standard enough by the Anglo radio professionals in Washington.[50]

Concerns regarding the lack of opportunities for Natives in the mainstream media were confirmed by a Broadcast and Cable Employment Report conducted by the FCC, which spanned a period of twelve years (1980 to 1992). Of all minority groups surveyed (females, Blacks, Hispanics, Asians, and Native Americans), Indian levels of employment were the slowest to rise, with gains that were almost imperceptible.[51]

Long-time Native broadcaster Susan Braine does not see this situation changing until some very fundamental questions of equality are addressed, "The fact is the whole industry is still controlled by white males. This is at the root of the problem. Until more minorities are accepted, the process will remain at a snail's pace, and Indians will be left out."[52]

## Chapter Four

# Talking Hogans: The Native Stations

---

Is it of men or gods who come out of the silence?
—Chippewa medicine song

## STATION OPERATIONS

At the time of this book's publication there were fewer than thirty Native stations licensed to broadcast, and another half dozen were in the process of getting ready to send signals in the air within the next year or so. Of these stations, only four (CKON, WASG, WYRU, and WOJB) broadcast east of the Mississippi.

Staff sizes of Native stations are typically small are but fairly consistent with Anglo stations serving audiences of comparable size. The number of full-time employees at Native stations ranges from two to fifteen, and volunteer levels at many stations run quite high, upwards of thirty. Reliance on volunteers is particularly strong at stations with smaller operating budgets.

All but three Native stations (KDLG, KABR, and KCIE) have ethnically diverse, or mixed, staffs. However, only four have staffs that are less than 50 percent Indian.[1]

The majority of Native stations serve rural audiences. "In some cases with scattered, low density populations (Ramah, Alamo) and in other cases fairly compact towns (Zuni)."[2]

*Talking Hogan* is an elder's term for a radio station building.

The rural nature of Native radio contributes to the medium's often obscure image in the mainstream community, believes Ray Cook. "Native radio exists in what has been termed 'extremely rural' situations. Often our geographic reality has been described by others as 'rural isolation.' These descriptions indicate a need to raise the profile and awareness of Native radio among our urban based contemporaries, rural allies, and the general public."[3]

While many Native stations enjoy extremely high listener loyalty, several battle for their audiences much like their mainstream counterparts. In fact, for many Natives, Indigenous stations are an alternative choice. According to Eiselein:

One of the mistakes that many radio station people (both commercial and public) make is to assume that their listeners listen only to their station and/or that they spend most of their time listening to their station. While Native American stations have extremely good overall listening (monthly, weekly, daily reach) and over half the population that they serve listen to the stations regularly, the Native American stations tend to be a secondary radio source for listeners.[4]

The monthly reach (the percentage of the population that tunes to a station) of Native broadcast outlets ranges from a high of 97 percent at KNNB to a low of 62 percent at KSUT, according to a survey of ten Native stations conducted by Eiselein.[5]

## THE STATIONS

What follows are profiles of noncommercial broadcast (and cable) facilities licensed to Native peoples. (Native stations with commercial licenses were described in chapter 3.) Most of the signals produced by Indians are sent from these stations, although not all Native stations are described here. They are presented in order of their date of license, beginning with the earliest.

Many of these profiles were prepared by individual stations especially for this book. They are presented almost verbatim and the author is acknowledged. Several profiles were previously published in *NFCB Community Radio News*. They are only slightly edited and acknowledgment is made. Other profiles are drawn from information generated by station or other sources.

## KYUK-AM/FM

The following profile was prepared by Jerry C. Brigham and Bruce L. Smith.

Radio television station KYUK in Bethel, Alaska, is a pioneer in Native American broadcasting and remains one of the most unusual and diverse public broadcasting stations in the system today. Built with a grant from the state of Alaska, KYUK radio first went on the air in 1971 and was followed two years later by KYUK TV. The stations were the first step in a plan that would insure a dependable broadcast service in a remote area of southwestern Alaska that had no chance of developing into a commercial market owing to a sparse population of Yup'ik Eskimos living throughout an area the size of the state of Ohio.

KYUK broadcast studios are located in Bethel, the largest city in southwestern Alaska, with a population of 4,500. The service area, reaching from the Bering Sea to the lower Yukon River, includes fifty-two Yup'ik villages. Bethel is the commercial hub for fishing, trapping, transportation, and shipping as well as headquarters for Native corporations, federal and state agencies, and health care facilities for the entire rural area. Located on the treeless tundra halfway between Anchorage, Alaska, and Siberia, Bethel is remote by anyone's standards; one must fly to reach it when the weather permits. Travel by truck is limted to a seventeen-mile loop of road, except in the winter when the nearby Kuskokwim River freezes solid enough to be declared a maintained state highway. All other transportation is by boat, dog team, or snowmobile. Whatever the means of travel, KYUK is the basic communication service for a community where the nearest movie theater, commercial TV station, and sports arena are 400 miles away.

Eighty-five percent of KYUK's audience is Yup'ik. Bilingual service has always been a primary goal of the station and takes the form of hundreds of hours of specialized local programs, which are aimed directly at the information and entertainment needs of listeners and viewers with no other local broadcast source. The station produces more bilingual Native-oriented programming than any other station in Alaska. Many anthropologists credit the availability of KYUK programming on a daily basis as being a major reason the Yup'ik language has stayed alive and prospered when many other Native languages have slipped into disuse.

Although KYUK is a fully qualified Corporation for Public Broadcasting station, which belongs and contributes to National Public Radio as well as the Public Broadcasting Service, as in urban stations, the majority of programs on KYUK are local in origin and uniquely designed to meet local needs. Disc jockeys play a mix of music that includes everything from locally recorded Yup'ik gospel to heavy metal. A unique feature of KYUK–TV is that it is the only public television station in the country with a waiver from the Federal Communications Commission that allows it to run programs from commercial networks as well as PBS. One of the most popular viewing periods features the *McNeil-Lehrer News Hour* programmed back-to-back with David Letterman; both may be interrupted by PSAs and station IDs in the Eskimo language.

The concept of a public broadcast station that is not an alternative service but simply the only service available places a huge load of responsibility on the facility. At KYUK, this translates into almost ten hours of local and regional news each week. Mornings on radio are filled with call-in bilingual talk shows, such as *Ask the Doctor*, *Yuk to Yuk*, and *Talk Line*. Another intricate part of the radio service in the bush of Alaska is KYUK's person-to-person message service called *The Tundra Drums*. Four times each day personal messages are aired; in many cases, the *Drums* may be the only way of communicating with a trapper, a fisherman, or a village nurse. The show also serves as an entertaining gossip line with its own set of code words.

Out of the necessity to air programming that is bilingual and useful to its Native audience, KYUK–TV produces several local series, such as a quiz show entitled *Ask an Alaskan,* a news magazine called *Delta Week in Review*, and a weekly horror movie series known as *Tundra Terror Theatre*. This brand of local TV, once common on small stations in the lower forty-eight during the 1950s, fits nicely with KYUK's original concept of community broadcasting.

In addition to being a unique broadcast service, KYUK also regards itself as an active collector of and depository for the oral and visual history of bush Alaska. The historical films and taped interviews in its collection number into the thousands and are prized and featured by such institutions as the Smithsonian and the Museum of the American Indian. Numerous KYUK documentaries give glimpses to the outside of the Native American cultures of the North.

Since its inception nearly twenty-five years ago, KYUK has grown to meet the imposing challenges of both serving and preserving a culture and way of life in a remote frontier environment. The small Native-owned and -operated radio and television station has, in many ways, set the standard for the Native electronic media that have since followed.

KYUK's general manager, John A. McDonald, describes the station's mission:

We supply educational, informational, and entertainment programming to the residents of this area. A vital service is our weather broadcasts. This is a very harsh climate, but people live off the land and are outside all year long. KYUK radio and TV also produces programs on health issues, Native land and political issues, and programs for youth. This area has had 20th century communications for only a couple of decades, and the residents now rely on the services that we provide. The stations provide a tool that local residents can use to explore the problems and issues that stem from the quickly changing lifestyles in this rural area. "Access" to this service is very important. The Native corporations from the various villages and the health services, school districts, and government agencies use this tool to reach everybody. The villages that surround Bethel have no plumbing, no roads, and they live with unsafe water sources. Communications funded by the State and Federal Government are vital as one way to try and keep these outlying areas in touch. It helps them respond and discuss their changing needs. What we provide is much more than "enhancing" to the local population. It is vital and saves lives. The information flows two ways, and the people have learned to use it both ways. I believe the area's residents would find it very hard to live without their one station.[6]

## KTDB–FM

The following profile was written by Bernie Bustos, former KTDB general manager.[7]

KTDB is located in Pine Hill, New Mexico, which is sixty miles southeast of Gallup. Pine Hill is a beautiful remote area that is at 7,450 feet elevation. KTDB serves the members of the Ramah Navajo community as well as others living within our forty-square mile area. During 1970, the members of the Ramah Navajo School Board, Inc., and the administration realized that effective communication with adult members of the community was an absolute necessity if the school was to realize its potential as a positive force in the area. The Ramah Navajo community was in need of technological advancement. Nearly 80 percent of the homes in the area were without electricity; nearly 98 percent were without telephones. There was virtually no TV reception and no local newspaper. The only link was an afternoon commercial Navajo program over a Gallup station and it really didn't serve the local need.

In the summer of 1971, the Ramah Navajo school board filed an application with the Federal Communications Commission to establish a non-commercial, educational FM radio station. During the winter of 1971, the license was granted and construction of the new broadcast facility began in Mountain View, New Mexico, a small village located eight miles north of our present studio. On 24 April 1972, KTDB was dedicated and became the first totally Indian-owned and Indian-controlled radio station in the country.

Because of the lack of electricity in many of the homes in the community, KTDB distributed 500 portable battery-powered FM radios throughout the community so the people would be able to hear the new radio station.

In the following years it became clear that a radio station that truly served the Ramah Navajo community would have to concern itself with more than school business. The services provided by KTDB have greatly expanded since its beginning. Programs in Navajo covering such subjects as health, sanitation, consumer protection, legal areas, and agriculture have become daily features. The community is kept informed on relevant government issues complemented by reports detailing the proceedings of Ramah Navajo chapter meetings, Ramah Navajo school board meetings, and daily reports during Navajo tribal council sessions. In addition, KTDB continuously promotes reinforcement and enrichment of local Navajo culture and values. Specific programs are devoted to Navajo tradition and history.

KTDB is funded by an annual budget provided by Ramah Navajo School Board, Inc., and grants received from the Corporation for Public Broadcasting. Because of our remote location there is no underwriting base to draw from, and pledge drives are not successful due to the current economic situation within the community.

I am very proud of our staff. There are six full-time and several part-time professionals. All but one on the full-time staff are Navajo, and all but two are women. The stability of our staff is the main reason for the station's success. The assistant station manager, Barbara Maria, is beginning her sixteenth year. The program director, Irene Beaver, is starting her thirteenth. Producer Lupita Adeky is in her twelfth year. Producer Martha Pino is in her sixth year, and the newest member of our full-time staff, Eral Eriacho, is beginning his fourth year of service.

The KTDB studio is now located adjacent to the Pine Hill School complex. We have a studio building that contains four offices, reception area, main control room, two production rooms, technical repair area, conference room, and small kitchen area.

Over the years we have been able to upgrade our equipment. We are currently working on obtaining some DAT recording machines as well as implementing a computerized programming system. Last year we purchased a digital editing system from Micro Technology Unlimited with the capability of editing programs up to an hour at 44.1 megahertz. We have also recently installed two backup generators. One is at our main studio site,

**Figure 4.1**
**KTDB Program List**

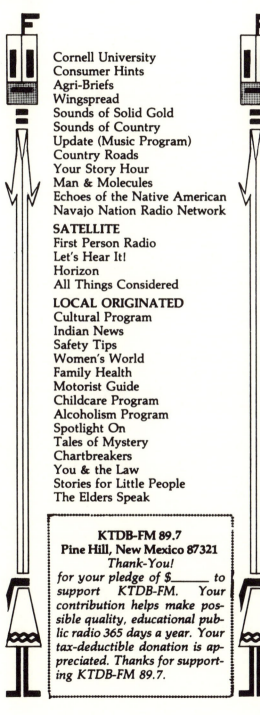

Cornell University
Consumer Hints
Agri-Briefs
Wingspread
Sounds of Solid Gold
Sounds of Country
Update (Music Program)
Country Roads
Your Story Hour
Man & Molecules
Echoes of the Native American
Navajo Nation Radio Network

**SATELLITE**
First Person Radio
Let's Hear It!
Horizon
All Things Considered

**LOCAL ORIGINATED**
Cultural Program
Indian News
Safety Tips
Women's World
Family Health
Motorist Guide
Childcare Program
Alcoholism Program
Spotlight On
Tales of Mystery
Chartbreakers
You & the Law
Stories for Little People
The Elders Speak

**KTDB-FM 89.7**
**Pine Hill, New Mexico 87321**
*Thank-You!*
*for your pledge of $_____ to*
*support KTDB-FM. Your*
*contribution helps make pos-*
*sible quality, educational pub-*
*lic radio 365 days a year. Your*
*tax-deductible donation is ap-*
*preciated. Thanks for support-*
*ing KTDB-FM 89.7.*

**Figure 4.2**
**Ramah Navajo School Board flow chart reflecting KTDB's position in the organization**

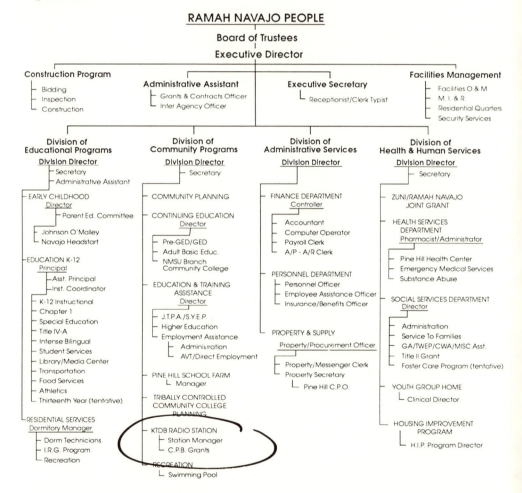

and the other is eight miles away at the transmitter. These generators will enable us to remain on the air during our frequent power outages.

The Ramah Navajo community has worked hard and the Ramah Navajo School Board, Inc. has invested well over $1 million and many years of development so that the people of the area can enjoy and benefit from a Navajo-owned and -operated radio station.

The commitment from individuals and licensees is what makes the difference between a station that succeeds or fails, and KTDB has enjoyed that commitment for the past twenty-one years.

KTDB and the Ramah Navajo school board have launched a project designed to provide broadcast training for high school students. Several students participate in the station's student volunteer training program.

The KTDB staff and management has formulated a number of locally originated programs that are designed to educate and inform in bilingual format. The KTDB production staff has the benefit of a fluency in both Navajo and English. KTDB caters to all age groups in the Navajo Community. *Stories for Little People* is a children's program that presents entertaining and educational stories. *The Elders Speak* deals with issues and problems that affect the elders of the Navajo people.[8]

The station's assistant manager, Barbara Maria, says that programming for the elderly is an important KTDB offering. "KTDB is especially geared to elderly Indians with only traditional values. This is a needed orientation. At the same time we attempt to address issues pertinent to all the age groups in our signal area."[9]

KTDB's program log reflects an abundance of local news and information features (most of which is broadcast in Navajo), tribal and top country music, traditional storytelling programs, and NPR shows, such as *All Things Considered* and *Morning Edition.*

An article of note on the early days of KTDB appeared in the *Journal of Broadcasting* in the summer of 1978. It was written by Stephen E. Rada, who examined the impact of the station on the residents of the Ramah Navajo Reservation. The study found that initially the station was as much a negative presence in the community as it was a postive one, since it failed to fully consider the potential effects of introducing a contemporary medium into a traditional culture—which had hitherto been isolated from the reach of most broadcast signals. Rada's research concluded that in its original incarnation the station promoted Anglo and mainstream values and ideals more than it did those of the Navajo culture, and this ran counter to the station's declared mission. The stations's present management believes that this is not the case today, if in fact it was the case during the early years of the station's operation.

## KOTZ-AM

Located twenty-five miles above the Arctic Circle in Kotzebue, Alaska, KOTZ-AM has been broadcasting its signal over a vast area of treeless tundra since 1973. It is the third oldest public station in the state.

At 720 kilohertz, the station has an effective radiated power of 10,000 watts, which gives it significant coverage. Says former general manager Bob Rawls (who has since moved on to Alaska Public Radio Network in Anchorage), "KOTZ serves an area approximately the size of Indiana, and we're the only signal out there, so listeners have but one option."[10]

The station's primary audience is Inupiaq Eskimo. However, it devotes only 12 percent of its airtime to Native-language programs. "That's because English is the dominant tongue in these parts now after the BIA's nearly successful eradication of the Inupiaq language. We still keep the language alive, though,"[11] observes the station's present general manager, Len Anderson.

Although it is an AM station, KOTZ is noncommercial and is funded by all Native-owned Kotzebue Broadcasting Inc. Its network affiliation includes Alaska Public Radio Network, Associated Press, and American Public Radio, which it recently switched to because it felt NPR was too expensive to maintain.

KOTZ's format is eclectic with a capital "E," says Anderson. "We really mix it up. Country, rock, classical, news, features—you name it. We have a huge audience to service, so we try to satisfy a diversity of tastes."[12]

## KEYA-FM

Licensed to the Turtle Mountain Chippewa tribe, KEYA–FM in Belcourt, North Dakota, operates at 19,000 watts from 88.5 magahertz and covers a radius of sixty to one hundred miles. The station began broadcasting in 1975. It serves between 8,000 and 10,000 people on and around the reservations (Turtle Mountain and Devils Lake Sioux), which are located just a few miles south of the Manitoba, Canada, border. It is in the geographical center of North America.

KEYA was the second public FM station to be licensed to a tribe, and today it boasts of the fact that it is the only Indian station managed by a female majority. "That's part of our pioneer spirit. We like to blaze new trails here at KEYA,"[13] says station manager Betty Hamley.

KEYA's programming is not directed primarily at Native Americans, but rather is a varied mix of elements. According to Hamley:

Our programming reflects our diverse listening audience. Our music format includes old and new country, old and new rock, fiddle, Native American, and spiritual music. We also have various programs aimed at various audiences, such as local and cultural programming, radio dramas, public awareness campaigns, as well as news and public affairs. We broadcast 19 hours a day (6 A.M. to 1 A.M.), except on Sundays when we sign-off one hour earlier (midnight).[14]

Only four hours weekly are set aside for Native (Etwaychik)-language programs, but the station devotes approximately twenty hours of its weekly air schedule to Indian-oriented features.

BIA Turtle Mountain Agency superintendent Dorene R. Bruce praises the station's programming efforts:

KEYA provides services to this Agency as well as other businesses on the reservation by announcing news releases, job openings, school closures, weather, and road conditions and other items of that nature that affect our daily lives. In our part of the country in particular, the weather and road conditon reports are vital to us during the winter months.(15)

## KDLG–AM

The following profile was written by KDLG's news director, Bob King.

Nestled deep within the Nushagak Bay area some ninety miles west of the entrance to the Alaska Peninsula, KDLG is a 10,000-watt, noncommercial broadcast station at 670 kilohertz. The station's signal is rebroadcast by four repeater stations in Alaska: KSDP at Sand Point, KIAL at Unalaska-Dutch Harbor, KUHB at Saint Paul-Pribilof Islands, and KNSA at Unalakleet.

KDLG is affilitated with the Alaska Public Radio Network, Associated Press, and American Public Radio. We're licensed to the Dillingham City school district, which is an elected group whose percentage of Natives and non-Indians varies. The station itself is in the process of forming a larger advisory board, which will more accurately reflect the Native community.

KDLG began broadcasting in 1975, the brainchild of a high school teacher who originally envisioned broadcasting classes to remote villages.

However, a more traditional format of music, news, and public affairs programming quickly emerged.

Located within the Dillingham high school building, KDLG conducts a broadcasting class as part of the school curriculum. Students who pass the course are eligible for part-time work at the station, and many have later gone on to receive full-time jobs at KDLG and other stations.

The station's broadcast area includes many Native communities, such as Aleuts, Yup'ik Eskimos, and Athabaskans.

KDLG covers Native issues in its news and public affairs programming and carries APR's *National Native News* daily.

Over the years the station has broadcast only a limited amount of Yup'ik-language programming, approximately 1 percent. The amount of Native-language programming has varied for a number of reasons, not the least of which has been the [limited] availability of translators and budget. Also while Yup'ik is the predominant Native language in the region, it is not exclusive to our broadcast area. Recently the station hired a special projects producer whose purpose is to focus on Native programming.

## KBRW–AM

Former KBRW station manager Bill Maines describes the station as follows:[16]

KBRW is community radio for the residents of Barrow, Alaska. KBRW considers itself the mirror of the people in the communities of the North Slope of Alaska. If all the residents of the North Slope looked into the same mirror at the same time, they would see what is being programmed on their station, KBRW. Our mission is to provide the people of the North Slope with quality service in providing information, cultural programming, and entertainment appropriate to our unique environment.

KBRW is an AM, noncommercial, community-supported radio station located in the northernmost incorporated city on the North American continent, Barrow, Alaska. The station broadcasts in English and Inupiaq with 10,000 watts of power at 680 kilohertz. A full-time staff of seven works eighteen hours a day, except during the whaling and hunting seasons when KBRW broadcasts twenty-four hours a day.

The station is owned, controlled, and licensed by its members, who represent 15.3 percent of the North Slope's population of eighteen and above.

KBRW owns and operates, with financial assistance from the North Slope borough, five FM translators via satellite in five of the eight communities we serve. The other two villages along with Barrow are able to receive KBRW without translator capability. The station installed three of the five translators thanks to a grant from the Public Telecommunications Facilities Program and donations from Shell Oil, ARCO, and BP Exploration.

KBRW has been on the air since 1975. The Alaska Educational Broadcasting Commission (AEBC) set aside $10,000 for a radio station in Barrow in July 1974. The same month, Silakkuagvik Communications, Inc., filed its incorporation documents. In 1975, $180,000 was made available for construction, and KBRW signed on the air on 22 December 1975, with $94,500 in annual operational support from the AEBC.

After ten years of operation in less than 1,000 square feet of space, KBRW moved to built-to-order facilities made possible by a capital grant from the Alaska Public Broadcasting Commission (APBC, formerly AEBC0). KBRW became CPB supported in 1984 and joined National Public Radio and American Public Radio in July 1985.

KBRW operates today with an annual budget of $700,000, a full-time staff of seven, a part-time staff of five, and ten volunteers. The budget is derived from grants from the APBC, CPB, the North Slope borough, and local fund-raising. The fund-raising budget includes proceeds from membership dues, underwriting, donations, premium sales, and bingo games.

KBRW's programming is as vast, diversified, and encompassing as the area it serves. Since it is the only continuous source of local programming for all the people of the North Slope, information is KBRW's most important product. This includes local and state news and public affairs, Native issues and interests, broadcasts of the borough governmental monthly meetings, public hearings and budget workshops, personal messages, and public service announcements.

Cultural programming is KBRW's second most important priority. The station is able to play a vital role in the preservation of the Inupiaq culture and language. KBRW is the only mass medium that can provide a significant program service relevant to the needs and interests of the Inupiaq people. The station is committed to presenting as much Inupiaq programming as possible. This includes Eskimo stories, music and dance programs, Inupiaq language and literacy programs, and special programs about the local culture. Local religious programs also serve an important role on KBRW by promoting shared values and strengthening ties among the North Slope people. In addition, KBRW does its best to provide as much bilingual programming as possible.

Entertainment is the third priority. As much as possible, KBRW feels that entertainment should amount to more than just filler material between

# Figure 4.3
# KBRW Program Guide

| Time | Monday | Tuesday | Wednesday | Thursday | Friday | Saturday | Sunday | Time |
|------|--------|---------|-----------|----------|--------|----------|--------|------|
| Mid-night | | | | | | | Blues Before Sunrise | Mid-night |
| 1 | | | Music Through the Night | | | | | 1 |
| 2 | | | | | | | | 2 |
| 3 | | | Local Music Mix | | | | | 3 |
| 4 | | | Monitoradio | | | Aggi | | 4 |
| 5 | | | Local Music Mix | | | Monitoradio | C.B.C. Sunday Morning | 5 |
| 6 | | THE EARLY EDITION National News Local News: 7:05 & 8:05 | | | | Local Music Mix | | 6 |
| 7 | | Sports News: 7:30 Current Events: 7:55 | | | | | | 7 |
| 8 | | National Native News: 8:30 APRN Statewide News: 9:05 | | | | Second Time Around | Local Music Mix | 8 |
| 9 | | | Local Music Mix | | | | We Like Kids | 9 |
| | | | | | | | Tell It... | |
| 10 | Parent's Journal | PSO Talk Show | Alaska Voices Live | Tusaayu-gaaqta Inuŋniñ | To Your Health | Discount Radio | C.B.H. | 10 |
| | | | | | | | Voice of Prophecy | |
| 11 | | | Local Music Mix | | | | Classical Showcase | 11 |
| Noon | | | North Slope News | | | Jazz Below Zero | | Noon |
| | | | Monitoradio | | | | | |
| 1 | | | | | | | Monitoradio | 1 |
| 2 | | | KBRW Country | | | Local Music Mix | Ang Inyong Lingkod | 2 |
| 3 | | | | | | | | 3 |
| 4 | | | Contemporary Music | | | American Top Forty | Music Mix | 4 |
| 5 | | | Alaska News Nightly | | | | Paglatisa | 5 |
| | | | Local Information | | | | | |
| 6 | | | Uqalugaat | | | | Record Shelf | 6 |
| 7 | | | Birthday Program | | | | Living Well | 7 |
| | | | Local Music Mix | | | 51% | | |
| 8 | Potluck | Brazilian Hour | KBRW Country | KBRW Blues | KBRW Rock | | Music Mix | 8 |
| 9 | Riders' Radio | 4 Queens Jazz | | | Aggi | KBRW Country Countdown | Arctic Inspiration | 9 |
| | Le Show | | Lifeline | KBRW Oldies | Grateful Dead Hour | | U.P.C. Choir | |
| 10 | KBRW Folk | KBRW Jazz | | | | | | 10 |
| 11 | | Music Mix | | KBRW Rock | | | | 11 |
| | | Baha'i Programs | | | | Music Mix | | |

informational and cultural programming. It should attempt to reflect the values of the high-priority programming by informing and bringing together the people of the North Slope. For example, we have a daily half-hour, live, call-in birthday program, a weekly one-and-one half-hour, live, call-in greeting program, summer broadcasts of local softball games, and winter broadcasts of high school basketball games.

Most of the programming described above is locally produced, which is often the most difficult and expensive type to produce. KBRW's ability to accomplish this is directly related to its staff, membership, board of directors, and community support.

KBRW has developed a Program Advisory Board with representatives from each of the villages it serves plus one member at large. This nine-member panel serves as an advisory committee for the program director. The committee meets quarterly and is charged with keeping written reports of conversations on KBRW's programming in between meetings. These reports will be used as a tool for changes or adjustments in the station's programming.

The station recently revamped its technical facilities. KBRW received a second PTFP grant. This one was approved for $255,025 to extend the station's tower to 400 feet and to purchase a new 10 kilowat transmitter. These improvements are designed to make KBRW's transmitting facilities reliable and efficient as well as to extend the signal to cover the camp sites used seasonally by residents for subsistence purposes.

KBRW devotes between twelve and fifteen hours of its weekly airtime to Native (Inupiaq)-language programs.

KBRW is carrying on a strong commitment to Inupiaq language programming. Not as a luxury, but as a crucial element in the survival of the Inupiaq culture. KBRW's collection of Inupiaq stories and legends has evolved through the years to over 180 hours of programming, many of which contain recordings of elders who have passed away. They speak in the old dialects and their voices continue to echo across the North Slope for all the children and adults to hear, learn and enjoy, every week night at 6:00 P.M.

Other Inupiaq language programs include Martha Aiken's

*Naalaqtuagaat* and the *Scripture Reading*. Both weekday morning modules provide early inspiration to listeners. Friday evenings bring an hour of celebration with *Agginaqsiruq*, Eskimo dancing tapes collected through the years by KBRW's live remote broadcast unit and produced for broadcast by Etta Ahkivgak Fournier.

Listeners also hear the Inupiaq language on programs such as our local public affairs programs, the *Birthday Program*, *Paglatisa*, some of the locally produced religous programs, and during weekday morning announcer programming. A new Inupiaq program, *Inupiaq Word of the Day*, hosted by Fannie Akpik, appeals to listeners whether they have been speaking the language all their lives or have just begun to hear the language. This is a program of learning and understanding.[17]

Says the station's current general manager, Don Rinker, "Native-language programming is a vital service, especially since 75 percent of our target audience is Eskimo. The balance of our audience is comprised of Anglos (12 percent) and Asians and Hispanics."[18]

During the summer of 1993, KBRW opened the Community Service Center in Barrow. The center serves as a public safety and public service information center for area residents as well as a store containing a variety of KBRW collectibles (mugs, T-shirts, pins, videos). The proceeds from the sale of these items help to defray station operating expenses.

## KSUT–FM

The following profile was provided by KSUT's communications director, Stasia Lanier.

KSUT public radio is owned and operated by KUTE, Inc., in afiiliation with the Southern Ute Indian tribe in Ignacio, Colorado. As the only Native American-owned public radio station in Colorado, KSUT has been in operation since 1976. What began as a 10–watt station broadcasting to Ignacio residents is now a 450–watt station that reaches across Four Corners.

KSUT is unique among Native stations because of its culturally diverse programming approach and the fact that it serves many Indian tribes, among them the Ute Mountain Utes and Southern Utes in Colorado, the Navajo nation in New Mexico, Arizona, and Utah, and the Pueblo Indians at Zuni Pueblo in New Mexico.

Southwestern Colorado has a very diverse non-Native American population as well, including fourth-generation Hispanic families, agriculturally based Anglos, oil and gas management and oil field workers, academic professionals teaching in the local college, and retired professionals making Durango their home for an active lifestyle of skiing, hunting, and fishing. Within this dynamic population, KSUT exists with minority programming (both syndicated and locally produced), NPR and APR programs, and music offerings such as jazz, classical, rhythm and blues, folk, classic rock, and blue grass. Native American programming provides a vital public service to KSUT's audience.

Staffed by five full-time and eleven part-time employees, KSUT broadcasts from the old Indian Health Center on the Southern Ute Indian Reservation in Ignacio. The board of directors is comprised of tribal members. The Southern Ute Indian tribe is a major business partner in the economy of the area. As stated by board president Eddie Box, Jr., "We are a progressive tribe that has preserved our cultural heritage while developing our economic resources."

KSUT is a source of pride and self-esteem for the members of the Southern Ute Indian tribe, as it provides quality programming and cultural awareness to the diverse communities in the Four Corners. KSUT is the only public broadcast format that is readily accessible. Public television is not available in Durango. The television tower was struck by lighting a few years ago, and the Albuquerque, New Mexico, station chose not to make the capital investment across state lines. KSUT is right there on the dial, but to tune into public television, a cable subscription is needed to get the Denver or Albuquerque stations.

People count on KSUT. Fort Lewis College in Durango has a tuition-free program for all Native Americans. These students come from across the country and appreciate the daily Native American programming. Newly relocated students are thrilled to find NPR news available in rural Colorado.

KSUT airs eight hours of Ute-language programming to area listeners, including the more than 2,300 Native Americans who reside on the Southern Ute and Ute Mountain reservations.

The station operates with six translators and is working toward upgrading the reach of its signal.

KSUT offers itself as a training ground for Natives interested in careers in broadcasting.

## KINI–FM

The following station retrospective was written by Father Joseph Gill, S.J., founder of KINI.

During the late 1960s, I was taking a summer course in the Community College at the University of South Dakota in Vermillion. I asked if it would be all right to do a study of the feasibility of a community college on the Rosebud Reservation as my research paper for the course. The professor agreed. My conclusion was that it was feasible; as a follow-up to the paper,

**Figure 4.4**
**KSUT Program Guide**

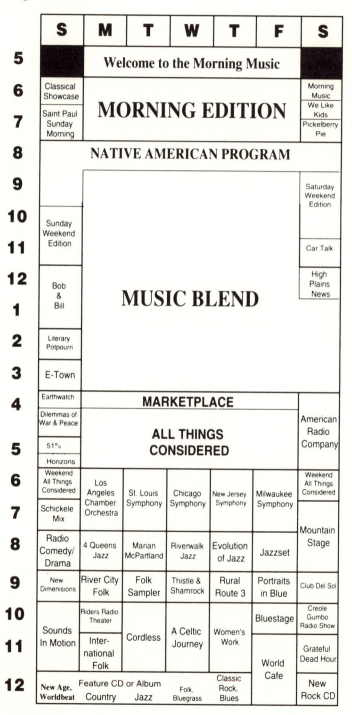

I tried to spell out a vision of how such a college might develop. Part of that vision was a college radio station. Through the efforts of others, the college (now Sinte Gleska University) did come to be. However, the radio station did not.

In the mid-1970s, St. Francis Mission (The Rosebud Educational Society Inc.) was in the process of turning over the school it has run since 1886 to a corporation of Lakota parents. The mission realized that the turn-over would free some resources to serve the people of the Rosebud Reservation in other ways. The idea of the radio station came up again. A committee of local people was formed (some of those involved were Manley Night Pipe, Dallas Chief Eagle, Angeline Rabbit—all now deceased—and Ben Black Bear, Jr.).

Father Bernard Fagan, S.J., then mission superior, assigned me to do some exploratory work while he sought some funding. Meanwhile, the committee was discussing the goals and objectives of such a station. Some of the goals they discussed: (a) the station would be a valuable means to dispel rumors (at the time, this was one of the primary objectives in the view of the committee); (b) the station would be a way to unify the tribe, to build community; (c) the station would transmit spiritual values—this group did not see any conflict between traditional Lakota and Catholic Christian spirtuality; (d) the station would protect and promote Lakota language and culture; (e) the station would provide a reliable source of local news and announcements of community events; (f) the station would provide education to community members—economic, health, political, child-caring, etc.; (g) finally, the station would provide culturally sensitive recreation— they wanted a strong component of traditional Lakota music and story.

The name *KINI* was proposed by Manley Night Pipe (who was the chair of the committee). Manley got the idea from the Lakota word for Easter. He felt that "kini" suggested the idea of new life, and that expressed in a nutshell their hopes for the station.

The following profile of the station was written by Bernard Whiting, Jr., general manager of KINI.

Radio station KINI is at 96.1 on the FM dial and operates with 57,000 watts of power. The tower is 350 feet high and is located just east of the station. There are seven full-time and two part-time staff—all American Indian. KINI began broadcasting in January 1978. The station is owned by St. Francis Mission.

**Figure 4.5**
**KINI Saturday Program Log**

```
12:00 am------WORLD NEWS, SPORTS, WEATHER.

 1:00am-------WORLD NEWS, SPORTS & WEATHER

 2:00am-------WORLD NEWS, WEATHER.

 3:00am-------WORLD NEWS, WEATHER.

 4:00am-------WORLD NEWS, WEATHER

 5:00am-------WORLD NEWS, WEATHER.

 6:00am-------WORLD NEWS, SPORTS & WEATHER & TODAY'S ANNOUNCEMENTS.

 7:00am-------WORLD & AREA NEWS, SPORTS & WEATHER. BIRTHDAY LIST & AA THOUGHT.

 8:00am-------WORLD NEWS, SPORTS & WEATHER & ALMANAC.

 9:00am-------WORLD NEWS, SPORTS, & WEATHER

 9:15am-------LOCAL SPORTS CALENDAR

 9:30aM-------CHILDREN'S BIBLE HOUR (29:30) (REEL.)

10:00am-------WORLD & AREA NEWS, SPORTS & WEATHER. BIRTHDAY LIST

10:30am-------PICKLEBERRY PIE (29:30) (CASSETTE).

11:00am-------WORLD NEWS, ☆ WEATHER

11:30am-------EARTH & SKY

12:00pm-------WORLD & AREA NEWS & SPORTS & WEATHER.

 1:00pm-------WORLD NEWS, LOCAL SPORTS CALENDAR, WEATHER & SPORTS UPDATE.

 2:00pm-------WORLD NEWS, AREA NEWS, SPORTS & WEATHER. BIRTHDAY LIST.

 3:00pm-------WORLD NEWS, STARDATE, WEATHER ☆ SPORTS UPDATE.

 4:00pm-------SPIN 180 (58:00) (CASSETTE) (SIDE ONE IS FIRST HALF)(SIDE TWO IS SECOND HALF).

 5:00pm-------WORLD NEWS, SPORTS & WEATHER.

 6:00pm-------WORLD NEWS, AREA NEWS, SPORTS & WEATHER & BIRTHDAY LIST.

 7:00pm-------WORLD NEWS, SPORTS CALENDAR, WEATHER  & SPORTS UPDATE.

 8:00pm-------WORLD NEWS, AREA NEWS, SPORTS & WEATHER.

 8:50pm-------STARDATE

 9:00pm-------WORLD NEWS, EARTH & SKY, WEATHER & SPORTS UPDATE.

10:00pm-------WORLD NEWS, AREA NEWS, SPORTS & WEATHER. AA THOUGHT.

10:20pm-------POWERLINE (29:30) (COMPACT DISC)

10:50pm-------STARDATE

11:00pm-------WORLD NEWS & SPORTS & WEATHER UPDATE.

12:00am-------SIGN OFF NEWS, SPORTS & WEATHER.
```

KINI serves the Rosebud Reservation and several white communities that surround the reservation. It's also heard on the Pine Ridge Reservation, mostly in its eastern and central parts.

We serve the Indian population by airing programs on the prevention of alcohol abuse, child abuse, and domestic abuse. We have a law show produced by the local legal services office in Mission, South Dakota. There's a quarter-hour program of powwow music and nontraditional Indian music that airs three times a week and features local and national Indian artists. KINI also produces a weekly news program on Indian news from around the country called *The Sicangu Chronicle*.

On Sundays we air several religious programs from the local churches. During the week a couple of the local churches have five-minute early morning programs. After 10 P.M. we have a rosary program from a national Catholic group. It happens to be one of the programs most tuned to by our older listeners.

KINI is on the air twenty-four hours a day, Monday through Saturday and 8 A.M. to midnight on Sunday. Country music is scheduled during the week from midnight until noon, and soft rock is aired from noon to 6 P.M. We program rock music between 6 P.M. and 10 P.M., and follow it with soft rock up to midnight. The weekend music schedule is similar, but we have an oldies soft rock music program on Sunday nights.

The station covers local events live whenever possible, and we brodcast several sports events from the two local high schools during the academic year. In addition, KINI broadcasts the rodeo live.

Our off-reservation listening audience is fairly substantial. It's primarily located in north central Nebraska. The people in that area say they like listening to KINI because of the large amount of music that we play and our noncommerical nature.

We get our world news off satellite from Associated Press every hour. Likewise, we get local news and weather from this satellite service.

## KSHI–FM

The following profile was written by Colleen Keane, a Native-station broadcaster.[19]

Tribally owned radio stations are offering a new sound on the radio dial—drum beats, powwow music, and Native American news stories of their own choosing. "It will be a new sound to your ears," says Arden Kucate [former station manager], of the Zuni radio station south of Gallup, New Mexico.

It is mid-morning, and *Native Drum Beats* is airing on KSHI–FM 90.9. When the Zuni corn dance fades out, Kucate turns on the microphone and in a deep, warm voice broadcasts several announcements in the Zuni language, which he then translates to English.

KSHI's radio waves travel down past the sacred war god shelter and the holy place known as Corn Mountain, then to the busy village where more than 10,000 Zunis, Anglos, and passing tourists tune in to 90.9.

"Most of the people walking around here listen to it. My radio is always tuned to that station. It tells you what's happening in the area," a community woman says as she hurries off to work in one of the many tribally owned and operated buildings.

Broadcasting both local and national stories, KSHI is the modern-day keeper of the land. Issues important to Native people are no longer over-looked or misreported, believes Kucate. Through KSHI, the Zuni people have been kept informed about the return of the Zuni war gods, about ceremonial pieces that were stolen from the Zuni pueblo, about a lawsuit that overturned a rancher's efforts to stop a pilgrimage that takes place every four years to the Zuni heavens, and about the recent ousting of Anglos from Zuni ceremonials because they ignored tribal directives.

Native American stations like KSHI air Zuni legends that were recorded by the old storytellers in the 1970s. Kucate is once again approaching the elders to document the Zuni legends, creation myths, and emergence stories. Kucate wants to record them so that these stories can be passed on to the young people of Zuni. It's part of our heritage and culture, and it will help to avoid identity crisis.

Throughout the day community people stop into the station to record a message or to drop off an announcement. A young woman, with a little girl tagging close behind, walks up to the control room and hands Kucate a piece of paper. "This is for tonight. Please announce it right away," the woman says. Kucate agrees in Zuni, and a few minutes later the community is informed about a vocational education meeting at the high school. It's not a response you would get from a commercial station in a big market. People come up to use the station because it's a free format, Kucate adds.

For non-Zunis, who often stop by the station to see if they are welcome on the reservation, KSHI aids their transition into Native culture by advising them of right and wrong behavior.

KSHI is situated across from the Public Service Hospital on a mesa in the Black Rock community. Its doors are open from dawn to dusk, Monday through Friday. If Kucate is not sitting at his desk, he can be found down the hall in the control booth. CDs, carts, cassettes, and records surround him in the studio, but no matter how busy things are, he finds time for visitors.

The KSHI building has been there for a long time. Now in his 30s, Kucate remembers laying the carpet when he was a teenager. That was in late 1970s. Then the station was buzzing with a full staff and several rooms full of equipment. Today, only a third of the house is used, and Kucate is a one-man team—manager, disc jockey, program director, janitor, and keeper of the lost and found cabinet.

KSHI has future plans to increase its power through additional transmitter sites. Several areas of the reservation, such as Nutria and Pescado, can't pick up the station's signal. If the station can get word out to the people in the sheep camps of bad winter storms, it could be life saving.

The station's music programming is as diverse as the community it serves. Zuni radio rocks in the afternoon with recent hit records and country and western favorites.

KSHI signs-off at dusk and signs on at dawn with traditional flute music by Native flutist Carlos Nakai. It's the station's way of expressing its appreciation to the sunrise and for another day of living, working, and communicating with people.

Since the preceding profile was written in 1991, there have been a few changes at KSHI, notes the station's current general manager, Duane Chimoni:

We have a staff of three who take care of the station's daily functions. Volunteers work our daily on-air block programming schedule, which features a variety of music, including oldies, contemporary hits, country, and of course both traditional and contemporary Native American music. Like any station, we have "canned" programs between the music. Operational funding of the station is provided through the Zuni Tribe under its general budget. A CPB sole service grant supplements that. Right now we broadcast with 100 watts of power, and offer between fifteen and twenty hours of Zuni-language programming each week.[20]

There are approximately 8,500 people residing on the Zuni Reservation.

## KIDE-FM

The following station retrospective was written by Joseph Orozco, former KIDE station manager and ICA secretary.

It was a Federal Register that got the attention of the Hoopa tribe [in Humboldt County, California]. In essence it said, you, too, can own a radio station. Send a letter to . . .

For years the tribe had wanted to pursue ways to promote the Hoopa language. When the Federal Register came across the planning office desk in 1978, they jumped at the opportunity. It was later learned how this notice came about.

The world of public radio has been dominated by the rich and urban since it was revealed that a radio station could be maintained on 2 percent of the per capita income of many larger cities. In the first ten years, stations were built by people who saw a means to provide alternative service to the public. However, the public that was served was the socially privileged. The weaker economic segments of society, mainly ethnic minorities, had little or no access to the electronic media. An attempt to address this disparity gave rise to the action of the FCC and NTIA, which offered specific numbers of noncommercial educational FM licenses to minority groups. Fourteen such opportunities were targeted for Native American communities. Ninety-eight Indian reservations applied.

The Hoopa tribe directed its education committee to enact the steps in the PTFP planning grant. Not knowing about the radio business, other than tuning in to one's favorite music, the committee hired a consultant to put together the PTFP construction proposal and the FCC license application. The scope of the plan was to build a 10-watt station for the primary purpose of promoting the Hoopa language. Complications soon followed.

The consultant had never built a radio station, yet still knew far more about radio than the education committee. A temporary studio was set up and students were placed in training slots from the tribal Comprehensive Employment and Training Act (CETA) program. Then the FCC changed the rules. Due to the proliferation of 10-watt stations, the FCC would no longer approve 10-watt applications. If any community wanted to pursue an FCC license, it must apply for a full-service signal at 100 watts or more. This was done and Hoopa was awarded one of fourteen construction permits to Native communities. However, social-political issues sprang up and the consultant was released.

NTIA was very concerned that Hoopa no longer had a consultant. They gave Hoopa the choice. If it wanted to continue the NTIA-funded process, it would have to hire a consultant who was suggested by NTIA. Hoopa obliged and KIDE-FM went on-the-air with 195 watts on 16 December 1980.

Orozco continues with a profile of KIDE.[21]

On 16 December 1980, at 10 A.M., a prayer was invoked by the spiritual leader of the Hupa people as the switch was thrown. KIDE, Hoopa, was on the air as the first and (so far) only Native-owned public broadcasting radio station in California.

KIDE is owned by the people of the Hoopa Valley tribe. As staff and management, we have worked through thin and thinner times to keep the station alive. Our reward has been, for the most part, moral support from the people of our community. We have asked the community for support, and it has been forthcoming. Payment of pledges has been quite high.

As the only radio station accessible to residents in eastern Humboldt County, KIDE is very important. The next nearest station is two mountain ranges and sixty miles away on the Pacific Coast. For years our rural communities have suffered from misunderstandings that were, in part, shaped by the other media located on the coast. We could understand how difficult it was for a reporter to travel all the way to our neck of the woods to find out the rest of the story and still make a deadline. So when the opportunity came along to fund and build a radio station, the Hoopa Valley tribe wasted no time in seizing it.

In the past ten years, the original goal of providing cross-cultural communication has been, as it continues to be, a major achievement. Stereotyped or untrue statements by Pacific Coast media about Native people or rural mountain communities can no longer stand without rebuttal. On several occasions KIDE has invited other local media staff to our studios to share with them reporting techniques and tips on how they can handle issues happening in the Hoopa Valley. These encounters are very helpful and are needed periodically as new reporters come into our region.

KIDE does not have a news staff. We would love to have one, and one of the mandates from our listeners is to provide local news. Thankfully our listeners understand the staff needed and costs involved in doing a credible job. We often hear comments about how much people would like to hear news, but these are usually qualified by "when you get enough staff." We have attempted to fill some of the gaps with occasional in-depth programs on important issues.

Information, education, entertainment, and the extension of our Native language—this is what we strive to provide to the local community. Within every live talk show or taped program we try to relate what each issue or action may mean to our community. We ask ourselves "What does this issue have to do with our people?" By using our own voices and by being true to our own identity, we add our Native feeling and perspective to every discussion.

KIDE has approximately ten people on its payroll and about as many volunteers. It offers a diversified format with about twenty hours a week set aside for Native programs. When surveyed in the early 1990s regarding Native-language programming, KIDE reported that it was not airing any.[22]

The Hoopa Reservation is home for 1,800 Native Americans.[23]

## WOJB–FM

Dave Kellar, WOJB program director, describes the station.[24]

The Lac Court Oreilles Indian Reservation in northwestern Wisconsin, where the "big pine" used to run dark to the horizon, is the home of the Lac Court Oreilles band of the Lake Superior Ojibwe and the home of WOJB, a 100,000-watt community station listened to by the tribe. Those humongous stands of big pine are long gone, but the indigenous people of the area are alive and well and playing powwow songs at 88.9–FM.

The station came on the air in April 1982, born of a perceived need to open up new lines of communication between the Indian and non-Indian communities of northern Wisconsin.

Racial tensions had sprung up in the wake of the new Indian activism that was blooming on reservations nationwide. Tribes were demanding their rights as sovereign governments, and state and local governments were saying "What?!"

On the Lac Court Oreilles reservation, tribal leaders and educators felt the increased polarization of the white and Indian communities was unhealthy for all involved and could lead to decreased tribal rights in the end. Communication between the cultures was considered esential to maintain a peaceful environment in northern Wisconsin. A basic problem perceived by the tribes was that whites in the community knew little about their Native neighbors. Out of these concerns came WOJB, a community radio station that ideally would help bridge the gap between the ideas and opinions to be aired. The station would also be a means for educating the people in the region on everything they ever wanted to know about Indians but were afraid to ask.

Although presenting the history of the region and its indigenous population is an important part of the station's mission, in their infinite wisdom the founders decided the station could also educate by presenting to the people in the woods of Wisconsin the best national programming available. We strive to present the widest variety of programming that our low budget can stand. We get news and plenty of it. News from NPR, news from APR, news from Pacifica, from the CBC, news from Indian country, from the old

# Figure 4.6
## KNNB Program Guide

### *SPECIAL PROGRAM BROADCAST*

Weekdays at 10:30, 11:00 a.m. and 6:00 - 6:30 p.m.

**MONDAY:** "NDEE" - Apache Culture program dealing with Native Indigenous issues.

**TUESDAY:** "EDUCATION AND YOU" - A series of weekly half-hour programs stressing the need and value of education and vocational training for both young and old. It will serve to encourage individuals to use education as a tool to improve life on the reservation.

**WEDNESDAY:** "TO YOUR HEALTH" - Weekly Health program. A weekly half-hour program presenting medical problems and health information of particular interest to the White Mountain Apache.

**THURSDAY:** "ISSUES AND OPTIONS" - Weekly program. Tribal leaders, tribal directors and staff speak to the White Mountain Apache Tribe on Social and Governmental issues facing the White Mountain Apache people.

**FRIDAY:** "FREE FORUM" - An open format program.

**SATURDAY:** "COUNCIL REPORT" - 10:00 - 11:00 a.m. An access program for the members of the Tribal Council to speak to the White Mountain Apache people on social and govern-mental issues. Re-broadcast 6:00 - 7:00 p.m.

*(Programs schedule subject to change)*

---

### *WEEKDAY SCHEDULE*
#### *MONDAY THRU FRIDAY*

A.M.

| | |
|---|---|
| 6:00 - 6:25 | Traditional Music |
| 6:25 - 6:30 | Arizona Radio News |
| 6:30 - 7:00 | Traditional Music |
| 7:00 - 7:25 | Country Music |
| 7:25 - 7:30 | Arizona Radio News |
| 7:30 - 8:00 | Country Music |
| 8:00 - 8:05 | K.N.N.B. News |
| 8:05 - 9:00 | Country Music |
| 9:00 - 9:30 | Children's Program (Summer only) |
| 9:00 - 10:30 | Adult Contemp. Music |
| 10:30 - 11:00 | Spec. Program Broadcast |
| 11:00 - 11:55 | Adult Contemp. Music |
| 11:55 - 12:00 | National Native News |

P.M.

| | |
|---|---|
| 12:00 - 1:00 | Oldies Show |
| 1:00 - 1:30 | Gospel Music |
| 1:30 - 2:00 | Indian Contemp. Music |
| 2:00 - 3:00 | Country Music |
| 3:05 - 3:05 | National Native News |
| 4:00 - 4:05 | Local News |
| 4:05 - 6:00 | Country Music |
| 6:00 - 12:00 | Rock Music |

1:30 - 2:30
6:00 - 7:00 p.m. Re-Broadcast
Tuesdays - Chairman's Report
An access program to speak on social and governmental issues.

1:30 - 2:30
6:00 - 7:00 p.m. Re-Broadcast
Thursdays - Vice-Chairman's Report
An access program to speak on social and governmental issues.

*(Time schedule subject to change)*

---

### *SATURDAY'S SCHEDULE*

A.M.

| | |
|---|---|
| 6:00 - 9:00 | Country Music |
| 9:00 - 10:00 | Adult Contemp. Music |
| 10:00 - 11:00 | Council Report |
| 11:00 - 12:00 | Adult Contemp. Music |

P.M.

| | |
|---|---|
| 12:00 - 2:00 | Oldies Show |
| 2:00 - 6:00 | Country Music |
| 6:00 - 7:00 | Council Report (Re-Broadcast) |
| 7:00 - 12:00 | Mix Format |

### *SUNDAY'S SCHEDULE*

A.M.

| | |
|---|---|
| 6:00 - 12:00 | Gospel Music and Religious Programs |

### *TELEPHONE NUMBERS*

| | |
|---|---|
| Fax Number | (602) 338-1744 |
| Request Line | (602) 338-5211 |
| Business Line | (602) 338-5229 |

country, news for Vietnam vets, news for computer junkies, news for real junkies, environment news, and much more, including our latest addition, *News That's Not*. This is a program that features the "best" of the tabloids, hot off the checkout counter.

The station's also famous for airing gavel-to-gavel coverage of interminably long judicial hearings, senate investigative hearings, and endless testimony on the confirmation of the White House cat. Day after day, the sound of shuffling paper challenges the stamina of even the most hardcore news junkie.

It's this kind of in-depth programming that makes WOJB stand out among the crowd. It's programming that has the local competition calling us kooks and weirdos. It's not too difficult to be an alternative radio station here in the midwest wilds where "Sandinista" is a four-letter word and your barber thinks Cokie Roberts is a wide-receiver for the Dallas Cowboys.

Speaking of sports, WOJB doesn't completely ignore them. Live coverage of the American Berkiebiner Cross-Country Ski Race is an annual frozen treat for us. In summer there's the Fat Tire Bicycle Race and Festival. Of course, the station's always ready to send a crew out for coverage of a good wood tick race or cat-staring contest.

News and information is the focus at WOJB, but there is music. In addition to the growing library of traditional and contemporary Native American music, we offer big band; bluegrass; bagpipe; reggae; rap; rock 'n' roll (in all its permutations); old folk; new folk; music from the nooks and crannies of the world, such as zydecko, salsa, tex-mex, and afro-pop; and some stuff that defies classification.

The station also sponsors music concerts featuring folk and blues artists of national renown. Greg Brown and John Trudell have been favorites since we began, and we were fortunate to have Bonnie Raitt and Lyle Lovitt do a benefit for the station this past year.

WOJB also broadcasts five or six powwows each year sponsored by tribal organizations, including the three-day Honor the Earth Powwow in July. This one draws an enormous crowd.

In summation, WOJB is a lot like the other members of NFCB—broke. The money thing. There's never enough—not for programming, not for equipment, and not for personnel. We're among the working poor, but we're smiling. Maybe because sometimes we actually do something here that makes a difference, for the good.

WOJB's station manager, Camille Lacapa-Morrison, adds the following comments concerning the station's programming mission:

The purpose of WOJB is to report on, participate in, and reflect upon all aspects of life in northwestern Wisconsin. WOJB seeks to inform its listeners of the significant issues facing society locally, regionally, nationally, and worldwide. The station seeks to increase participation in public broadcasting through programming and training, volunteer activities, community events, and outreach services.

An important part of WOJB's mission is to reflect credit upon the Ojibwa and other Indian Nations and to promote harmony and understanding between the Indian and non-Indian communities within its service contours and other areas of influence on the national level. Since signing on, WOJB has become a bridge between two cultures.[25]

## KNNB–FM

The following profile was written by Sharon Harris, former station manger of KNNB–FM.[26]

On 11 September 1982 KNNB began broadcasting on the Fort Apache Indian Reservation, home of the White Mountain Apache tribe, which encompasses approximately 1.6 million acres in the exquisite White Mountains of north central Arizona. Whiteriver is the seat of the tribal government and it is located 184 miles northeast of Phoenix, the capital of the state. There are approximately 10,000 enrolled members of the tribe and 1,000 nonmembers on the reservation.

KNNB—Apache Radio, began transmission with 630 watts of power on 88.1. The station facility was funded by the Housing and Urban Development (HUD) community development block grant and the equipment was purchased with NTIA/PTFP grants. KNNB employs seven full-time people, who are White Mountain Apache. The tribal council of the White Mountain Apache tribe provides funding for salaries and operation of KNNB Radio.

The primary mission of KNNB, Apache Radio, is to provide for the first time a local broadcast service to the residents of the Apache Reservation. The majority of the population of this area are Apache tribal members. KNNB is committed to providing programming in both the English and Apache languages. The station's daily fare includes locally produced programs, such as the following:

*NDEE* is a weekly Apache culture program that captures the unique cultural, linguistic, and historical background of the White Mountain Apache people. This program increases the cultural identity of the White Mountain Apaches and improves the overall understanding of the tribe's culture among the surrounding nonreservation communities within KNNB's coverage area.

*Education and You* is a series of weekly half-hour programs stressing the importance of educational and vocational training for young and old. It serves as a vehicle to identify job opportunities as well as to encourage individuals to use education as a tool for the improvement of life on the reservation.

*To Your Health* is a weekly health program presenting medical problems and health information, especially alcoholism and drug abuse, of particular interest to the White Mountain Apache.

*Issues and Options* is a weekly program by tribal leaders, directors, and staff speaking to the White Mountain tribe on social and governmental issues facing the White Mountain Apache.

KNNB's schedule includes country, adult contemporary, oldies, traditional Apache, and religious music. The station also airs plenty of news and information programs sensitive to the needs of the Apache people. KNNB provides live and recorded coverage of civic and governmental events as they occur throughout the reservation.

Phoebe Nez, KNNB's current station manager, expands on the station's mission and goals:

Apache Radio endeavors to keep area citizens informed as to local governmental and civic affairs and to provide a platform for the discussion of issues of local concern or controversy.

It is the goal of Apache Radio to provide coverage for all reservation communities. This not only includes the main population centers of Whiteriver and surrounding communities but also the remote reservation communities of Cibecue, Cedar Creek, Carrizo, Hondah, McNary, and Foresdale. Apache Radio has as a goal the continual upgrading of service and quality of programming. Programs produced will capture the unique cultural, linguistic, and historical background of the White Mountain Apache People.[27]

KNNB reaches approximately 18,000 people, more than half of whom are Native Americans. The station sets aside between six and ten hours of its weekly on-air schedule for Native-language features.

## KILI–FM

KILI (*Kili* is the Lakotan word for "special") is one of Native broadcasting's unique stories. It was conceived by AIM supporters out of frustration with the absence of adequate communications on the Pine Ridge Reservation in Porcupine, South Dakota. "During the reign of terror from 1973–75, the reservation had no local media that AIM could use to spread information."[28]

KILI began broadcasting in February 1983 in commemoration of the tenth anniversary of the occupation of Wounded Knee and the seige at Oglala in which several people (both Indians and non-Indians) were killed. The clash between AIM supporters and federal agents at Wounded Knee in the early 1970s harkened back to the massacre eighty years earlier in which hundreds of Sioux lost their lives.

Nearly twenty years after the occupation at Wounded Knee and a century after the "great and terrible slaughter" there, KILI (which stands a few miles to the north of the site) became the center of yet another clash between Indians and whites.

In 1990 a non-Indian, Tom Casey, was hired as KILI's acting station manager. When he made changes in the broadcast schedule a couple of years later, which terminated the services of an Indian staff member, trouble broke out. According to Casey, in the spring of 1992 he ended the regular broadcasts of a station staff member, who he felt was using the airwaves as a soap box to convey her personal views on issues regarding the reservation. This dismissal he considered an appropriate action given the declared mission of the public radio station, which is licensed to an independent broadcast entity (Lakota Communications), whose goal is to provide fair and impartial programming for all members of its listening audience.

The day following the firing, Casey was confronted in his station office by the disgruntled former employee, her husband (a prominent member of the reservation's tribal council), and members of the local AIM chapter (according to Vernon Bellecourt, the national chapter of AIM regarded this incident as an internal affair and so kept out of it). When Casey refused to reinstate the canceled program, the terminated employee struck him in the face with her fist.

Soon the reservation police were involved and Casey was being escorted daily to his office past a protest camp (referred to as a spiritual camp by protesters), which set up its headquarters in the station's front yard. The camp remained in place until the frigid winds of winter arrived, at which time the issue had lost considerable steam, since Casey's actions had been upheld by several courts, both tribal and otherwise.

During this time, Casey's opponents had argued that the station belonged to the people of Pine Ridge, having been created for them by AIM, and therefore it should be returned to them and not run by an outside corporation and a non-Indian.

Casey's life was threatened on several occasions, but he steadfastly held to his belief that KILI was not there to serve the exclusive agendas and goals of a particular faction or group. "Since this is a public broadcast station and not owned by the reservation tribal council, it is here to serve all the people without prejudice, and that is what it does. I wasn't hired by the reservation, so I can't be fired by it,"[29] said Casey.

Looking back on the situation, the executive director of the Pine Ridge tribal council, Mike Her Many Horses, supports Casey's stand. "He was justified in doing what he did. He was attempting to preserve the integrity of the station's program mission."[30]

Delbert Brewer, superintendent of BIA's Pine Ridge Indian Agency, gives his perspective on the controversy:

The hostile situation that arose from the KILI encampment was originally staged as a protest against alleged injustices rendered by the KILI Board of Directors. Subsequent issues that arose from the encampment were not related to the original issues of dissatisfaction with KILI Radio and the Board of Directors. This led to a confrontation between the encampment "powers that be" and the tribal government. The issues eventually evolved into a threat by the encampment to overthrow the Oglala Sioux Tribal government. The encampment was eventually disbanded by the Oglala Sioux Tribal Courts on the basis that the camp was a political camp and that as such it was in trespass on tribal trust land. Mr. Severt Young Bear, the original leader of the camp, died a few months after the incident. Gary Rowland represented the local AIM chapter and was very active in the encampment.[31]

As of this writing, Casey remains at the helm of KILI, although the Lakota Corporation has advertised for his replacement, specifying a desire to hire a Native American.

KILI operates with 100,000 watts of power, making it one of the most powerful Native stations in the country and a substantial presence in a state whose Native population constitutes 10 percent of the total. KILI's signal covers 30,000 square miles and is assisted by six translators. The station is on the air daily from 6 A.M. to midnight and airs nearly thirty hours of Lakota-language programs each week. About a third of its broadcast schedule is devoted to Native programming. The station airs a mix of country, rock, and Lakota music, a heavy schedule of public affairs and community features, and local and national news and sports. Seven paid employees comprise the station's core staff, which is augmented by several volunteers. A third of the station's funding comes from CPB with the balance derived from many fund-raising events, underwriting, and various other donations. Its annual operating budget exceeds $300,000.

Dale Means, KILI's first manager, says that the station has operated under a stigma that has sometimes detracted from its accomplishments: "When the station first went on the air, the headline in the Rocky Mountain News read "Terrorists Erect Radio Station." From the start the station has provided total open access to the people it serves as well as honest, accurate information so vitally needed to mitigate tensions. KILI has been an instrument of good in the community and has helped the cause of Native public broadcasting."[32]

Although steeped in political intrigue since its inception, KILI is among Native broadcasting's most-listened to frequencies. The station claims that 95 percent of reservation residents tune it during the course of a normal day. "That's impact," says Casey.

## KMHA–FM

Nina Fox, station manager of KMHA–FM, provided the following profile.[33]

KMHA–FM is located at 91.3 and its studios are approximately five miles west of New Town, North Dakota. On your way to KMHA you'll cross the mile-long Four Bear's bridge, which goes over Sakakawea and leads into the Four Bear's Park.

When you enter the park you'll see our Tribal Administration Building, Four Bear's Gas Station, Four Bear's Museum, our Tribal newspaper office, and a few yards behind an Earth Lodge, KMHA.

The "HMA" stands for the Hidatsa, Mandan, and Arickara tribes, the three affiliated tribes of the Fort Berthold Reservation. During the 1950s, the Garrison Dam was built on the Fort Berthold Reservation. The Missouri River flooded the fertile valleys where our people used to live. The federal government relocated our people to five separate segments on the benchlands above the river. The benchlands are windswept prairies where it is difficult to grow crops. Our people were fragmented, and many ceremonies and cultural activities were lost.

Disillusioned, many turned to alcohol and developed chronic health problems. Because the tribal council recognized the need to bring our people together and to stimulate the culture, KMHA was created.

KMHA serves several very remote rural communities on and near the Fort Berthold Reservation, which is geographically divided by a 155,000-acre reservoir. KMHA provides the vital link necessary to transcend the geographic barrier and distribute important community information. Outside of its tribal listeners, KMHA also serves a significant audience of Scandinavian descent, which helps generate cross-cultural understanding.

KMHA has five full-time staff members and one part-time employee. All station staff members have on-air shifts, including the station manager. We're all active in producing programs, too.

The station's programming consists of community reports five times daily, plus informational, educational, and entertainment programs broadcast throughout the day. KMHA's morning begins with the sign-on, flag song, and prayer aired in all three traditional languages. The station airs Native American songs throughout Indian country and local cultural programs on the three tribes. National programming can be heard in the evenings.

This year the staff tried a new fund-raising event centered around the tradition of personal honor songs, which are composed in recognition of individual tribal members who are the center of a significant event or contribution. KMHA focused on local war veterans, those killed in action or currently serving our country. These songs are cherished by the individual and his family and can be sung only by the one who composed the song or by the drum group that knows the honor song and only at the request of the honored individual or his family.

KMHA took pledges and requests from listeners, and the songs were rendered live by our local drum group, the Mandaree Singers, in the station studio. This became a special two-day Memorial Day tribute to our veterans of Fort Berthold. This was the first time such songs have been rendered for broadcast. In deviating from the traditional use of these songs, the staff had to structure the programming to be very culturally sensitive.

We realized that these personal honor songs can be forgotten if they aren't repeated. Some of the requests could not be rendered because the singers had forgotten the songs.

The response was overwhelming. Elderly people in particular were very supportive of this effort. The Memorial Day tribute netted more than eighty-five pledges ($3,000) and was the most successful on-air fund-raising event in KMHA history. Particularly encouraging was the high degree of community support and recognition the listeners gave to the people of the Fort Berthold Indian Reservation.

The KMHA program director and long-time veteran of the station Pete Coffey, Jr., adds these details to the profile. "The station's prime age group is 25 plus. We're a 100 kw operation that airs a diversified format, but we go very heavy on Native programs. Our staff is 90 percent Indian."[34]

Fort Berthold Agency BIA superintendent Terrance Walters gives KMHA high marks for its service to the community:

KMHA has provided valuable services to the reservation residents. Fort Berthold Reservation is approximately 48 miles wide and 42 miles long, which equals 415,427.16 acres. The approximate mileage mentioned does not include the highway system from one community to another. Distances enrolled members have to travel to another community for services or activities [are] lengthy and time consuming. The radio station provides tribal members public service announcements, upcoming cultural activities, tribal news, health information, and so much more. The list is endless. Its services are very important. Since all communities are in remote areas, its programming saves people travel time and money.[35]

## KABR-AM

The following profile was written by Linda Middleton, former KABR station supervisor.[36]

In 1983 the Alamo Navajo School Board, Inc. (ANSB), on the Alamo reservation in New Mexico, built the community radio station (KABR-AM) through the National Telecommunications Information Agency. Since that time, funding for staffing the radio station has been through various Department of Education training programs. The station's focus in its beginning years was aimed at providing communication to the Alamo community regarding ANSB programs, special announcements and events, changes in schedules, and so on. Electricity came to Alamo only in 1982 and telephone service began in 1986, so our signal primarily reached cars and trucks of Alamo residents.

In 1988, ANSB submitted a proposal for a discretionary grant to the Office of Indian Education (Department of Education) for a communication arts project. Included in the grant proposal was a budget for a broadcast arts instructor who would train Alamo students in radio journalism and broadcasting, provide career awareness in the broadcast arts, and increase English oral-language development.

KABR turns into a radio lab on Tuesdays and Thursdays. Grade school and high school students take part in the lab. They are taught how to operate equipment, produce programs, and speak on the air. The students are also encouraged to develop programs in the Navajo language, which helps them develop literacy in their own language as well as English.

Tuning to KABR, listeners may hear a grade school student reciting a Native American poem, a junior high school student reading the community news, or a high school student hosting a locally produced show, like the *"Dedication Hour"* or the *"Alamo Children's Show."*

KABR has also developed its own local programs, which feature the children of Alamo, the elders of Alamo, community news from around the area, special reports, Native American programs, and a parents' show. Local programming is broadcast in both Navajo and English.

In the past years, KABR has received several grants to do special programs. Two programs, "Fetal Alcohol Syndrome" and "Navajo Women as Leaders," were produced and broadcast through a grant from the New Mexico Women's Foundation. The New Mexico Endowment for the Humanities has sponsored a program called *Alamo Place Names*, which is currently on the schedule. In addition, there is the Johnson O'Malley program, in which staff from the Head Start Program and KABR co-produced weekly shows utilizing *Sesame Street Magazine*. Three- and four-year-olds on the reservation receive monthly subscriptions to the magazine and the staff produce programs directly relating to articles in the magazine.

Funding the operations of the station is the biggest challenge. The funding for public radio stations usually comes from community businesses and listeners. Indian reservations, especially ones as remote and poor as the Alamo reservation, do not elicit such support. Most of the people of the Alamo band live at or under the poverty line. Since the signal does not reach to Socorro or Albuquerque, the closest urban areas, it is difficult to convince businesses to become underwriters.

KABR administration continues to search for other sources of underwriting and support. The Indigenous Communications Association, of which KABR is a member, is a coalition of Native stations that is developing funding sources for Native radio. KABR is currently vying for operational funding through the Navajo nation and the state of New Mexico.

To date, the development of Native radio has been difficult. Stations have struggled with limited funding and little or no broadcast training. Yet they have survived through community support and involvement. KABR is no exception to this. Development has been slow, but through the perseverance of staff and community, the station continues to blossom and grow.


KABR, refered to as K-Bear (not to be confused with the fictional station depicted on TV's *Northern Exposure*) by most staff people and listeners, is presently managed by Patsy Apachito. It broadcasts from 1500 kilohertz with relatively low power and offers a mixed format that includes twenty-five hours of Native-language programs each week. The reservation served by its signal has a population of approximately 1,300.[37]

## CKON–FM

Kallen M. Martin, general manger of CKON–FM, wrote the following profile.

CKON is located in the Akwesanse Reservation on the international border between Quebec Province and New York State. Our listeners live in an area ranging from Chateauguay, Quebec, to Massena, New York, and from St. Regis, Quebec, to Cornwall, Ontario. On good-weather days, we broadcast even farther. We currently have a 350-watt transmitter. However, with the equipment we have, CKON has an approximate 650-watt-effective radiated power level.

The station serves its community through the community calendar of events, which is aired four times daily, Monday through Friday, and twice on weekend days. The community calendar lists events and activities sponsored by local programs and organizations, for example, Head Start, senior citizens associations, recreation departments, tribal council, band council, traditional council, schools, and so on.

Since we don't have a news department as of this time, we occasionally do updates on issues specific to the Akwesasne. For instance, over the summer and early fall there was a lot of shooting, centered on smuggling activities, on the St. Lawrence River, the major waterway through our territory. We helped the council and police department (Canadian side) produce a public service announcement calling for an end to the shooting in the name of public safety.

Anther example of CKON public service focuses on health in Quebec. In 1993 the Quebec government voided Akwesasne residents provincial health insurance. They assumed Akwesasne residents in Quebec were really New York state or Ontario residents trying to get health insurance through Quebec. We produced a public service announcement for the council and health personnel about what measures were being done to rectify the situation and what residents needed to do to have their health costs covered.

More recently, the gaming compact signed between New York governor Mario Cuomo and two of the three St. Regis Mohawk tribal chiefs (American side) has been widely discussed by various groups in the community. CKON produced a public-service announcement bringing the community up to date on the compact and its implications. Given the enormous impact the agreement has on our community and what it means for all Akwesasne of both sides of the border, we hope to do more as developments occur. Unfortunately, not all groups involved have responded to our requests for information, so the station can only air what it gets or what the groups wish aired, provided it does not reflect badly on one group or another.

In other areas of our programming, we provide Akwesasne businessess with the opportunity to advertise on our airwaves. (CKON is permitted to set aside a limited amount of its airtime for commercial messages, because it is licensed by the Mohawk nation council of chiefs and is not eligible for government funding.) The station offers Native-owned businesses a 15 percent discount on its advertising rates. CKON has a policy of not accepting advertising from establishments that are in business to sell alcohol. At the moment, Native-owned businesses constitute less than half of the station's advertisers. Non-Native advertisers are located in Cornwall, Massena, and Malone.

During the summer, CKON employs students through a Canada Employment Center program. Occasionally we have training programs for Akwesasne who are interested in production and deejaying. Last year, we started radio bingo, which serves as a fund-raiser for the station. Numbers are called out in English and Mohawk and about nine games are played. As a way to help other community groups, a tenth game is played. Half the proceeds of this last game go to the group that requested financial assistance and the other half goes to the winner. From 23 November 1993 to 17 May 1994 approximately $8,500 was raised.

Depending on the availability of funds, CKON has plans to return Mohawk-language instruction to the airwaves. The program would be about an hour long and broadcast weekly.


Former CKON station manager Ray Cook expands on the origin of CKON and its unusual licensing arrangement.

SEKON (CKON) was built when Akwesasne Freedom Radio (AFR) went off the air. The money to build this station ($25,000) came through our treaty with Quebec. Immediately the Canadian federal government required SEKON to apply for a license to operate. The traditional Mohawk council of chiefs began negotiating with the Candaian Radio Television Corporation (CRTC) for regulatory rights. Since the Mohawks already had radio, the CRTC avoided confrontation by recognizing the Mohawks' ability to regulate the station's operation. Through its government and treaty relationships, the Mohawk community at Akwesasne and its projects remain eligible for Canadian government grants. The United States does not quite see it that way. Private foundations are another source of revenue.

SEKON's building is situated, like the rest of the reservation, half in Canada and half in the United States. The broadcast booth is in Canada, and

**Figure 4.7**
**CKON Program Information**

FORMAT

| | | |
|---|---|---|
| Country Music: | Monday through Friday | — 6am to 3pm |
| | Sat/Sun | — 8am to noon |
| Rock or Pop: | Monday through Friday | — 3pm to 6am |
| | Sat/Sun | — 12pm to 8am |

Specialty Shows

| | | |
|---|---|---|
| | (Teen music/information Show) | |
| | Thursday | — 5pm to 6pm |
| "State of Rock" | (Hard Rock): | |
| | Saturday | — 8pm to midnight |
| "Roots of Rock" | (Blues Show) | |
| | Sunday | — 8pm to midnight |

Community Service Programs

| | | |
|---|---|---|
| CKON Auto Shop | Aired daily | — 8:30am, 4:30pm |
| Job Watch and Trading Post | Aired daily | — 10:30am |
| Nat'l Native News | Monday to Friday | — 11am, 4pm, 8pm |
| Community Calendar | Aired daily | — 9am, noon, 3pm, 6pm |
| Pet Corner | Aired daily | — 2:30pm |
| 51% (Women's Show) | Tuesday | — 12:30pm |
| Environment Show | Wednesday | — 12:30pm |
| Health Show | Thursday | — 12:30pm |

the antennas and tower are in the United States. The transmitter sits on the dividing line between the two countries. The FCC does not recognize SEKON. This means that neither do the federally funded agencies (CPB, NPR, APR, NAPBC, etc.). This lack of recognition is disturbing, since SEKON services the U.S. side of the reservation and the outside white communities.[38]

## KCIE–FM

The following profile was provided by KCIE station manager Warren Cassador.

KCIE in Dulce, New Mexico, began broadcasting on 3 December 1990. But for a few minor interruptions, we've been on the air since. The station's power is 100 watts, but our antenna is high on a mesa, so it increases our coverage area significantly, almost sixty miles. KCIE was extablished primarily to provide education and information communication service to the community of Dulce and the Jicarilla Apache Indian people.

Our goal is to help preserve the traditional culture of the Jicarilla Apache and to maintain a solid Native foundation in the area. We are presently working with the elders of the community on storytelling and Native-language lessons.

KCIE broadcasts eighteen hours a day throughout the week and devotes about 20 percent of its air schedule to Native-language programming. Our overall orientation is Native programming. One of our popular daily features airs mornings and is called *Native Drum Shot*. The station is multiformatted and eagerly anticipates the launch of the American Indian Radio on Satellite (AIROS) project, which it plans to join.

The station is licensed to and funded by Jicarilla Communications. We're not affiliated with any network because we haven't had a satellite dish to get their signals, but this situation is soon to change because a dish is about to go up. We'll carry APR when this happens and be on-line with AIROS too.

KCIE works closely with the youth of the community on a number of different programming projects. We're a community station in the truest sense of the term.

In their research on Native radio stations in the early 1990s, Jerry Brigham and Bruce Smith found that the subject of Native-language programming at KCIE was one that aroused diverse opinions: "At KCIE, Apache-language programming is a touchy issue. The language is considered sacred, and the issue of broadcasting in Apache has not been fully resolved by the community and station. While broadcasting in Apache would seem to contribute to the preservation of the language, its broadcast transmission makes some people uncomfortable."[39]

Station manager Cassador says that while this unease may have been true a few years ago, the station has gone to the other extreme and now does everything it can to get the language out over the air as a means of preserving it. "Saving the language is central to our very mission as a public station, and everybody in the community pulls together in this effort."[40]

## KGHR–FM

The following profile was written by KGHR's station manager, Stu Schader.

KGHR is a 100-watt station licensed to the Tuba City High School Board, Inc., in the Navajo nation. It operates out of Greyhills high school, in Tuba City, located on the eastern edge of the Painted Desert in north central Arizona. Its signal reaches approximately 16,000 listeners. KGHR is the nation's only Native American high school radio station.

We have a very diverse audience in regard to age owing to our unique mix of programming. As a noncommercial educational radio station, we have a dual purpose. We are here first to train Native Americans in radio broadcasting and second to serve the community with news, information, and entertainment.

Our target audience mornings is the twelve to forty-nine age group. From 6 A.M. to 8:30 A.M. we air NPR's *Morning Edition*. KGHR is an associate member of NPR; that is, we repeat the signal of a member station and so avoid paying an affiliate fee. Between 8:30 A.M. and 11:30 A.M. we air country music. Then from 11:30 A.M. till noon we broadcast *Arizona Edition*, which contains news and information for the state. In the afternoon and evenings our target audience is twelve to thirty-five. From noon to 5 P.M. we air a mix of music that includes rock, pop, reggae, blues, Native, and variety. Between 5 P.M. and 6:30 P.M. NPR's *All Things Considered* is aired. After that, we're all music up to sign-off at 11 P.M. We strive to be a community service, and approximately 30 percent of our programming is based on Native concerns.

KGHR is preparing to acquire down-linking capabilities through a PTFP grant. This grant is being coordinated with NAPBC, ICA, and AIROS. Once the dish is in place, the station will apply for a national program and production acquisition grant (NPPAG). This grant is given to public radio stations that have down-linking capabilities and tune to the public radio satellite. The current funding amount per year is $12,500. The grant is used to purchase and distribute national programming.

KGHR is an associate member of NPR through a repeater agreement with KNAU in Flagstaff. In an unprecedented move, KGHR is seeking dual associate status via an agreement with KJZZ in Phoenix. This would give us the opportunity to repeat two NPR member stations. If approved, KGHR will be the first radio station in the nation to attain dual associate member status with NPR. The primary reason for repeating two member stations is that KNAU does not provide overnight programming and KJZZ does. As I said, it is the goal of KGHR to serve its community with as much quality programming as possible.

## KCUK–FM

KCUK–FM station manager Peter Tuluk provided the following account.

A federal grant of $95,000 put KCUK on the air in 1990. The station serves three communities: Chevak, Hooper Bay, and Scammon Bay, Alaska. The people in these communities are predominantly Cup'ik or Yup'ik Eskimos, and the majority of them speak their Native language. For that reason the station devotes the majority (75 percent) of its on-air schedule to Cup'ik-language programs. Our programming mission is to reinforce the value of the Cup'ik way of life.

KCUK operates in the village of Chevak on the edge of the Bering Sea. At the present time the signal is 10 watts, but we hope to get it up to several thousand watts by sometime in 1995. We operate with an annual budget of about $100,000, which comes from our licensee, the Kashunamiut school district, and state grants.

We're on the air from 9 A.M. to 9 P.M. Monday through Friday and a little later on the weekends. We repeat the broadcasts of Bethel station KYUK so that our listeners get comprehensive regional, national, and world news coverage, which we're unable to provide, since we don't have a satellite dish. We hope to get a dish eventually.

We recently did a telephone survey in which we asked our listening audience what they thought of KCUK's programming. It was gratifying to hear the responses, which were almost unanimously positive and supportive.

KCUK has two full-time employees and three part-timers. We have a large complement of volunteers, who are very important to our operation.

We're here because we believe in what KCUK represents to the people of the lower Yukon and Nelson Island areas.

## Channel 20

Cable television programming created by Natives for residents of the Lower Brule and West Brule Reservations in South Dakota can be accessed on Channel 20 by Sioux Satellite Cable Subscribers. Channel 20 began feeding its signal to Lower Brule viewers in 1991. It is operated by Bill Ziegler and several volunteers and offers local programming five days a week between 1 P.M. and 8 P.M. Regular features such as *Eltwin Grass Rope*, showcasing area talent; the *Scott Jones Show*, focusing on Indian issues and affairs; and *Lower Brule Children's Hour*, funded by the Christian Children's Fund, are among viewer favorites.

According to Ziegler, the channel evolved to address the specific needs of the reservation. "Information seems to get twisted before it gets to its recipients. So Channel 20 is here to get accurate information out to the reservation. It's also here to fulfill the needs of Lower Brule children. Channel 20 is very children oriented."[41]

Channel 20 is funded by small grants and out-of-pocket contributions. Supporting the channel's operation has been an ongoing challenge, says Ziegler, who overall is optimistic about the channel's continued operation. At the present time, the cable channel is searching for other sources of funding.

## Channel 56

Known affectionately as "Purple Cow TV," because it was the only low-power television application granted and accepted during the LPTV freeze of the 1980s, Channel 56 is licensed to the Rock Point school board in the Navajo nation. On the air since April 1987, its signal is confined to the Rock Point reservation.

A grant from PBS got the channel operating, and subsequent federal funding has kept it running, says Janet Sauer, a teacher at the Rock Point Community School, who coordinates the station's programming efforts:

An NTIA/PTFP grant of $53,000 gave the Rock Point community of about two thousand Navajo people the opportunity to gain information and share ideas about the world. The senior class here produces high quality video tapes, primarily documentaries and educational training tapes, which have been aired on Channel

56 and on KOBF-TV in Farmington [New Mexico]. We are arranging to air our shows on the Navajo Nation TV station in Window Rock, Arizona, and we hope to have NAPBC distribute them. We repeat PBS signals for our viewers. My predecessor, Eleanor Vilarde, had great difficulty in getting the PBS signal rebroadcast via Rock Point. Finally, she was able to get the signal from KUED, Channel 7, out of the University of Utah in Salt Lake City. The signal is sent over six different translators, and we often have technical problems during bad weather. Channel 56 began rebroadcasting PBS on 9 May 1990. It was an important event here.[42]

Purple Cow TV's signal covers a twenty-mile radius, which until the channel's debut was untouched by any television signal. "The area is in a valley, so before we went on the air residents needed a satellite dish to get TV reception," says Sauer.

The station's staff consists of Sauer and Rock Point Community School students, who combine their efforts to originate two hours of programming each week, including a one-half-hour news show, that is designed to stimulate discussion on local issues within the community. The rest of the station's airtime is filled with pre-recorded material.

Channel 56 has no budget, per se, notes Sauer, who says that she is compensated for her efforts through a Title 5 grant, which pays her for teaching the station's students but not for running the video operation. "We're actually looking for the Navajo Nation to assume financial and operational responsibilities of the broadcast facility. There are plans through the School and the Nation to build new studios. We believe that as we become more bilingual there will be a greater interest in funding the operation. Time will tell."[43]

The Rock Point community television station is licensed by the FCC as an educational low-power TV operation, and as such it is not permitted to air commercial material, although on-air program underwriter attribution is allowed.

Sauer is optimistic about the future. "We've been a long shot from the start. We weren't suppose to get on the air in the first place. That's why they call us 'Purple Cow TV.' "[44]

The station's slogan, "May the Purple Cow walk in beauty," seems to suggest that positive forces may well inform the operation's fate.

## NNTV–5

Navajo Nation Television in Arizona can be seen via cable on Channel 5. It has been sending a signal down the coax line to nearly 5,000 subscribers since the late 1980s. The channel re-airs PBS broadcasts and each week originates five hours of local programming, which is directed exclusively at Navajo viewers. These programs focus on topics that have particular relevance to the lives of reservation residents.

NNTV–5 has plans to offer its signal on the UHF band, says its director of broadcast services, Delfred Smith. "This will make our programming more accessible to folk who don't want to get involved with cable hookup. It's an important step in fulfilling our mission to serve the needs of our people."[45] The move to UHF was planned for the summer of 1994.

Other Native stations, such as radio stations KHAC in Window Rock, Arizona; KUHB in St. Paul, Alaska; KIYU in Galena, Alaska; KSW in Sisseton, South Dakota; and KNSA in Unalakleet, Alaska, as well as LPTVs and cable channels (Blackfoot Tribe TV in Montana and Cherokee Cable in North Carolina, among others), serve their Indigenous constituencies in much the same manner as those stations depicted in this chapter.

## Mixed Bloods: KSKO–AM

An interim category of Native stations exists, which is sometimes re-ferred to as "mixed bloods." These are stations that may be classified as Native-owned and -operated at certain times and not at others. Such stations have boards that often alternate between being predominantly Native to predominantly non-Indian, or Anglo, depending on the outcome of elec-tions. This situation is particularly common in Alaska.

An example of a mixed blood station is KSKO–AM, which at the time of this writing had a majority Native board. An election was slated for the following fall, which could change the makeup of the station's governing body. Situated in the heart of the Kuskokwim Mountains in west central Alaska, KSKO broadcasts from McGrath, a village of some 600 residents. At 870 kilohertz, KSKO went on the air in July 1981 and is licensed to Kuskokwim Public Broadcasting.

The station radiates 10,000 watts and operates with two repeaters for expanded reach. It claims roughly 5,000 listeners in an area about the size of the state of Minnesota, according to its program director, Doug Letch, who comments on the station's programming. "We really air a mixed bag of things here: rock, country, reggae, classical, jazz, Native, blues, and oldies. You name it we play it. We're very eclectic in order to satisfy so many different tastes."[46]

KSKO is affiliated with APR, AP, and APRN Radio and airs news throughout the day, devoting over twenty hours a week to information programming. It derives its operating funds from a variety of sources, namely CPB, APBC, and local underwriting and fund-raising efforts. A significant amount of its support comes from its membership pool.

The station carries *National Native News* and a few other Native-oriented programs, but despite the fact that its audience is comprised largely of rural Eskimos, it does not offer any Native-language programming. According to Letch, the station has determined that few of its listeners really converse in Eskimo or Indian tongues. "English is the predominant language here, so we haven't felt particularly compelled to air anything else."[47]

Former KSKO station manager Susan Braine says that as far as station listener loyalty is concerned, that depends on a number of factors. "Like anywhere else in broadcasting, it really depends on if there's anywhere else to tune. I would say that a tribal station is typically the listening choice for people on a reservation, but up here that's not the situation really. Stations like KSKO that have a vast coverage area with non-Indian potential listeners/supporters program for a more general audience.[48]

As with most stations in vast remote areas, KSKO plans to add additional repeater sites to reach unserved listeners. When this happens, the amount of Native programming may well increase.

## Chapter Five

# Waves for Kekewh: Impact of Indigenous Broadcasting

The Voice—our Voice—is getting stronger
Rising to the turquoise sky—
Listen! You will hear it soon . . .
Very soon . . .

—Carla Willetto,
Navajo

## A VITAL PRESENCE

There is little to dispute claims that Native stations have contributed to life in the Indigenous community. In this chapter representatives from many different sectors of Native America comment on the impact of Indian-operated electronic media operations. Much of the information herein has been culled from questionnaires and interviews with tribal members and officials, BIA agents, Indian scholars, and broadcast professionals, as well as from in-house audience surveys prepared and administered by individual Native stations. This chapter does not purport to be a scientific analysis of Native broadcasting's influence but rather an informal assessment and overview of the way Indian stations have or have not made a difference in the communities their signals serve.

In the opinion of those responding to the question "What is Native broadcasting's foremost contribution to the Indigenous community?" the

*Kekewh* is the Powhatan word for "living."

dissemination of accurate, honest, and relevant information (that which has specific and poignant value and meaning to reservation residents) ranked highest.

In *Bury My Heart at Wounded Knee*, author Dee Brown quotes Yellow Wolf of the Nez Perce tribe as saying, "The whites told only one side. Told it to please themselves. Told much that is not true. Only his own best deeds, only the worst deeds of the Indians, has the white man told."[1]

To the Indigenous population, Native media provide a significant opportunity to get the other side of the story told, something that mainstream media have been slow in doing.

According to Father Joseph Gill, founder of KINI-FM on the Rosebud Reservation:

In contrast to "mainstream media," Native American broadcast outlets are able (to the extent that they do not let themselves be co-opted by "mainstream" values) to be clear voices for the people and culture they represent. They are free to express the values of their own unique cultures in both their Native language and in English. They are free to provide a forum for the expression of their needs and desires. They are free to provide public service announcements and other information important to their listeners. In short, they can be a liberating and creative force in their mission to get the "word" out to their communities.[2]

Information about things directly affecting the lives of Indians was extremely scarce in many Native communities prior to the advent of Indigenous radio. Getting the word out was difficult. Many of these areas were not even served by mainstream broadcasters. Today, Native stations often are the only communication sources available to thousands of Native Americans.

In a recent edition of the *Arizona Republic*, writer Jerry Kammer observed, "Radio is the dominant means of communication on a reservation where most families don't have telephones and many live in the sort of spectacularly lonely canyon butte and mesa country that has shaped the world's images of the Wild West."[3]

In her report on Native American radio for NAPBC, Nan Rubin made the following observation:

To places like Pine Ridge, South Dakota; Zuni, New Mexico; and Ignacio, Colorado, the reservation radio stations are the only media available. There are no daily papers, few or only long-distance radio station signals can be heard, and they are often too far away from reliable television signals. The public radio service is the only reliable means of communicating timely news, public service announcements, and information to area residents.

On many reservations, there is very limited telephone service. The public radio stations provide emergency information and announcements in the most efficient manner possible.

Entertainment opportunities in these rural areas are limited. The stations provide entertainment for people in their homes, and also serve as sponsors for such activities as teen dances, sport and civic events, and cultural celebrations. Broadcasting these activities brings them to the entire reservation, not just the people who are able to attend.[4]

Peterson Zah, president of the Navajo Nation, sees Native radio as an indispensible means of communications for his people. "On many reservations these stations are the only communication companies that reach out to the Indian people. In the Navajo Nation, radio is the primary form of communication. It would be difficult to exist without it."[5]

Existing without Native media would reimpose hardships that would make life even more difficult in Indian country. Stations such as KILI have become the bedrock of the Lakota Native American community, says public radio station manager Anna Kosof. "It is the voice of a community where phones are scarce and the listeners turn to KILI for essentials of survival, whether blankets on a cold night or community news."[6]

Native broadcasting gives listeners a chance to become aware of the events that affect their lives. "There is often an interest in local and national politics because the outcomes of the races affect tribes very directly—whether the candidate will be good or bad for the interests of the tribe. This is very important,"[7] says Rose Robinson of the National Congress of American Indians.

Indigenous media is perceived as a way to address significant problems existing on the reservation. "Native media can help to solve problems through the distribution and sharing of information within and between Native communities."[8]

Leonard Burch, chair of the Southern Ute tribe, believes that connecting Indians with the world is a service for which Native stations should be praised. "They do a real good job informing the tribe on issues and events, either local or far away, that will or may have an influence on the way it functions in life."[9]

Alex Lunderman, president of the Rosebud Sioux tribe, conveyed similar sentiments to KINI upon the occasion of its tenth anniversary on the air. "The station's service to the community is immeasurable, and I want to

**Figure 5.1**
**Note: Percentage indicates the number of Natives on the reservation who tuned into stations.**

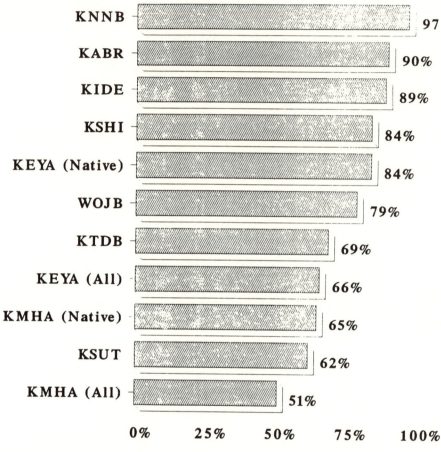

May-June 1992 Surveys by A & A Research

*Source*: Reprinted with permission by E. B. Eiselein

encourage it to be a trendsetter for Indian radio communications. In KINI we surely do have something to be proud of."[10]

Agents of the Bureau of Indian Affairs uniformly hold that Native broadcasting contributes to life on the reservation and in the Indigenous community. "The local station here has been very effective and long overdue in our community. Its impact has been positive. It has opened the lines of communication. We now have up-to-date information on community events and national Indian issues. Our awareness has been raised,"[11] says Marvin

Molson, acting superintendent of the Jicarilla Agency in Dulce, New Mexico.

About KILI, BIA superintendent Delbert Brewer contends that "The presence of the radio station has had a positive impact on the residents of the reservation. There is more information available about crucial health concerns and local political issues."[12]

Regarding KEYA, Turtle Mountain Agency superintendent Dorene R. Bruce notes that despite the presence of Anglo media, the Native station has filled a formidable void with its targetted programming.

Although there are television as well as radio stations which the local community has access to, I believe that for the most part we rely on our local Indian station for news relative to our daily lives. For example, due to our close proximity to the Canadian border, our weather conditions are affected by the Canadian fronts that are monitored by our station. KEYA also announces Native American news, which we can't receive from the other local stations. Legislation affecting the Native American is also only broadcast by the station. So the local Native station provides services to the community that it would not otherwise have access to if it had to rely on other radio and television stations.[13]

The Three Affiliated Tribes of the Fort Berthold Reservation have been uniquely and effectively served by KMHA, observes the agency's BIA superintendent, Terrance Walters. "The station has provided a great deal of needed services to the Indigenous people of this area. Things have changed for the better because of it."[14]

In surveys conducted by several Native stations, listeners stated that the information they receive from these facilities makes a difference in their lives. "Surveys are valuable for Native stations, because they, more than any other, want to be in touch with their audiences. Our surveys have encouraged us to do what we do,"[15] says KTDB's Barbara Maria. The station offers the following listener statements as representative responses to recent surveys:

From my point of view, the radio station is really important for the community. Most everyone gets their information from it.

KTDB gives us what we need to know in the community.

At KTDB, you can understand the announcer. The updated information is good.

It has friendly, personal deejays. We support our radio station. We asked for a station. We got one, and we like it.

The educational programming is excellent.

I like everything about KTDB.

The service the station gives us is very important. It does a good job.

Bob Sommer of KIYU explains the surveying approach his station employs to ascertain the likes and dislikes of its listeners.

We gauge how we're doing by two methods. First, we send out a survey every couple of years and usually get about a 25 percent return. There is a comment section on the survey, and it's rare to get a negative comment. Second, our membership drive is held once per year. We've been able to expand every year because our membership has also. It has not only kept up with the cost of living but exceeds it. We do take all comments and suggestions we receive seriously. Some of the responses have bettered the station. Our members and listeners know this, and they know we're receptive to their suggestions and observations.[16]

Not all comments are favorable, says Sommer, who offers a couple by way of example. These were made in a KIYU survey taken in the early 1990s.

I would like you to consider *not* playing the music of all animal rights activists on your station. There is no reason you should promote their music when they are so drastically affecting the economy of rural Alaska. You should have a *no play policy* for such people as Paul McCartney, K. D. Lang, and John Denver, to name a few. Also you should tell the listening audience the reason for not playing their music. These people are adversely affecting everyone in the north who lives a rural lifestyle. They are out of touch with reality, and their motives are 100 percent self-centered and based on emotionalism, not facts. Please reply. I will not join your station until you make a policy.

I listened to the recent series of basketball games which Galena City schools played in Kaltag. I am very concerned about the negative statements which were made about the Galena team and their coach by your announcer. I consider it inappropriate and detrimental to the image and reputation of our school for the announcer to continually make derogatory statements about our players. I sincerely hope that future games will be announced in a manner which will not embarrass our community.[17]

According to Sommer, comments run at least 90 percent in favor of the station's programming. He cites the following statement in a KIYU survey (by an official of the Department of Interior's Fish and Wildlife Service) as a more typical response to the station's broadcasts:

Thank you for the live broadcast of the Federal Subsistence Meeting in Galena. I am sure the broadcast helped the public keep informed of this complicated and changing issue which is so important to local area residents. I feel that continuous communication on this issue will be vital to community understanding of the issue and to our obtaining meaningful public input. We have always appreciated the station's efforts in informing the community of important local events.[18]

The majority of surveys conducted by radio stations, both Native and mainstream, are anything but scientific. What they do is provide stations with a useful impression of the efficacy of their programming endeavors as perceived by their listening clientele.

Robin L. Claymore, administrator of the Office of Planning and Economic Development for the Cheyenne River Sioux tribe, says that to ascertain the impact of Native broadcasting on the Indigenous community a more formal approach is needed.

To determine the impact on Indian Society and Culture that can be directly attributed to the availability of broadcast information one would have to have an example and a statistically significant sampling of the population both before and after a station goes into operation. As with any society the dissemination of information directly related to the listening/viewing audience will have an impact on both society and culture. As to the nature of that impact, it would seem reasonable to assume that as with any society, the more information available to the population the better decisions can be made in areas that affect lifestyles.[19]

Formal audience research employing the methodology cited by Claymore is seldom found in Native broadcasting, if it is found at all in mainstream broadcasting.

## A Unifying Force

Native stations have brought the Indigenous community together. They have reduced the fragmentation and scattered nature so characteristic of Indian country. This is particularly true on large reservations, such as those of the Papago and Navajo, says E. B. Eiselein. "Radio can allow people in the outlying areas to 'tune-in.' In a place where physical access to the remote areas is difficult (even for four-wheel drive vehicles) and time-consuming, Native radio offers an opportunity to transcend these barriers and unify the people."[20]

Native stations provide a strong identity for the reservation, says Nan Rubin.

The stations are able to break down barriers which exist between the reservation and the off-reservation community. They are a strong vehicle for educating non-Indians about the history, culture, conditions and activities of reservation population.

They are able to share cultural values, experiences, and events, making them accessible to listeners. By broadcasting in Native languages and focussing on local customs and practices, they reinforce the value of tribal cultures and the identity of Indian people. At the same time, by broadcasting positive images, they can counter many of the negative racist stereotypes held by non-Indians.

The stations also broadcast news, information, and other programming relating directly to the needs and concerns of reservation populations. This gives legitimacy to these concerns and strengthens their importance, especially when they are not addressed by any other media.

They have a unique identity. The reservation-based public radio stations are special in the public radio arena, because they represent a particularly unique and little understood segment of American ethnic culture. Given the opportunities, they see themselves as being able to share their own concerns with each other, and also bring their little-heard voice to the greater public radio audience. They are a terribly undervalued resource which has the potential for elevating our national understanding of and appreciation for Native American people.[21]

Rubin contends that Native stations represent a source of pride for their people, because they are positive examples of how Indians can directly benefit Indians. "The radio station can be a very public, visible accomplishment, which is seen as a high source of pride. It legitimizes the concerns which Indian people have and serves as a public statement of self-determination.[22]

Evelyn James, president of the San Juan Southern Paiute tribe, agrees with Rubin's assertions, adding, "These stations are important symbols of Native self-actualization. Yes, they do make an important statement."[23]

Native stations are capable of bringing tribes together as well as connecting individuals on reservations. "Radio can be a Pan-Indian force. While tribes maintain a strong sense of tribal identity . . . , radio can bring these groups together for their mutual good," observes E.B. Eiselein.[24]

In part the pride that Indians feel for their stations stems from the employment opportunities and training programs these stations offer. Given the lack of jobs on most reservations, the positions and employment assistance these stations make available helps address a crucial problem.

In her report for NAPBC, Rubin found the following:

1. Every reservation-based radio station provides paid employment for at least one to five full-time positions.

2. At CPB-qualified stations, five or more positions are in place, which is a considerable number of paid employees.

3. These jobs often provide personal motivation and pride for the people filling them. The jobs are real, concrete work, which are made evident in the community just by turning on the radio. They provide people with real skills which can also be used off-reservation.[25]

The training Native stations provide constitutes an invaluable resource for the Indigenous community, but it is often hampered by a lack of proper funding and necessary expertise. Rubin makes the following suggestions in her report as a means for addressing these issues:

The radio stations are some of the strongest, most creative reservation enterprises, which provide challenging, productive work for employees. But learning the necessary specialized radio skills is difficult with the limited resources available in most reservation environments.

1. Some station staff members have learned their skills off-reservation in school, at other jobs, or at other radio stations, but the largest number of staff is untrained when they come to the station. The reservation-based stations need to know about the range of training opportunities for all skill levels and positions which are available through the public broadcasting system.

2. Scholarships and other kinds of financial support should be made available to assist stations in sending staff to training activities.

3. The stations should be assisted in setting up staff exchanges, station visits, and other vehicles to facilitate sharing human resources and expertise among themselves.

4. Efforts should be made especially to strengthen the skills of station managers, including participation in structured management training workshops, conferences, and regular interaction with the managers from other stations.[26]

Since the preceding report was written in 1987, some of these measures have been implemented, aided greatly by the efforts of ICA and IBC.

## A Preserver of the Indian Way

Indigenous broadcast stations are an important factor in the preservation of Indian culture and language. This is the opinion of Native and non-Native peoples alike, many of whom believe this to be Indigenous broadcasting's single most important contribution and its raison d'être.

Today Indian traditions are no less threatened by cultural imperialism than they have been in the past, but with the growing number of Native stations, most of which strive to highlight Indian culture and language in their program schedules, the chance of survival has been enhanced.

The absorption or annihilation of Indian ways by the mainstream is at the very least allayed by the efforts of Native programmers and producers. NPR news reporter and former Native broadcast station employee Corey Flintoff appreciates the role of Indian media as cultural guardians. "These stations play a vital role in personal identity and cultural preservation. This is what makes them unique. It is their defining contribution to the world."[27]

Flintoff's former employer, KYUK in Bethel, Alaska, has been honored for its contribution to the preservation of its area's Indigenous tongue. "The station's been cited several times [for] saving the Yup'ik language. By using the language daily, KYUK keeps the tongue alive and helps it spread. News done in Yup'ik helps keep the old words alive and helps introduce people to the more technical 'new' words of the language."[28]

Native radio language and culture broadcasts teach a younger generation about the ways of Indian life past and present, observes E. B. Eiselein. "Native radio can be a teacher to the young. It can teach language, both Indian and English, as well as other subjects. Radio can be a cultural force. It not only can reinforce the existence of Native language, but it can also teach it to a whole new generation. For example, KILI taught listeners Lakota at Pine Ridge. Native radio can help keep music and stories alive too. Some stations air powwows."[29]

AIM's Vernon Bellecourt is gratified to hear traditional music over the radio. "It's really good to be driving down the highway and hear traditional Indian music. Where else would you hear it, if not from Native radio?"[30]

Native writer Luci Tapahonso reflects on what hearing traditional music over the radio meant to her: "While we ate breakfast, my father watched news, the table radio played Navajo and English songs alternately. . . . The songs that the Yeibicheii sang, that the radio played, and that my mother hummed as she cooked are a part of our memories, and our laughter."[31]

Curley Biggs, president of the Ramah Navajo tribe, says that Native radio's broadcasts of what is unique in Indian history make it a very important service. "It really benefits the community. Programs with the tongue and the traditions reach large audiences. This is very good, especially for the elders, who use nothing but Navajo to communicate."[32]

Without language broadcasts, thousands of Native Americans would live without a connection to the outside world. "These broadcasts in the language mean a great deal to the tribe and Indian culture. They guarantee a future that is mindful and appreciative of the past which possesses the key to what we are,"[33] notes Alfred Trepania, vice chairman of the Lac Court Oreilles tribe.

Native broadcaster Patsy Apachito says that listeners within the reach of her station's signal depend on the language broadcasts. "There's very limited reading of the English language here, so without our language broadcasts many people would not know what is going on in their community. Without us, all our audience could get would be the Anglo's broadcasting from Albuquerque."[34]

KTDB's Barbara Maria comments likewise. "The majority of reservation inhabitants do not understand other languages [than] their own. Many of them are uneducated and the station is their only source of information about what is happening around the world and also where they are living."[35]

Native-language programming embraces present-day themes as well as traditional ones. For example, KTNN airs Phoenix Suns basketball games in the Navajo tongue, which is a cousin to the Athabaskan and Apache languages. The live broadcasts are popular throughout the station's signal area, which covers the entire western third of the country.

Despite the presence of Indian stations, the language and culture of Native Americans continue to be the target of mainstream animosities. This disapproval adds to the importance of the role of Indigenous media, says Eiselein. "They are a first line of defense in many respects. There are still calls for the 'termination' of Indian tribes, which includes stripping Indian nations of their lands, their cultures, their languages, and their religions."[36]

Perhaps when all is said about the role of Native media, the bottom line will be that it has made existence on the reservation more tolerable, says Peter Nabokov. "Among the forces that enliven Indian reservation communities are Native media, especially radio and newspapers. Families enjoy powwow music and Indian language shows over these reservation airwaves."[37]

## CRITICISM OF NATIVE STATIONS

Native broadcasting is not without its critics. Complaints about these stations often run about as high as those for mainstream stations. Among the most common criticisms of Native stations is their lack of sufficient language programming.

Mike Her Many Horses, executive director of the Pine Ridge tribal council, feels that Native stations can do more in this area. "From what I've heard, there really could be more on-station language education than there is. More occasions of Sioux-language programs would be beneficial to both those who are fluent in the language and those who are not familiar with it."[38]

His sentiments are prevalent in other areas served by Native broadcast signals. For example, at KTDB it is not unusual for survey participants to cite a lack of language programming in response to the question "What, if anything, do you dislike about the station?" Ironically, KTDB offers more Native-language programming per week (ninety hours) than does any other Indian-operated radio station. At some stations, there is a desire and even a plan one day to broadcast entirely in the Native tongue of their listeners.

Many in the Native community would like to hear more programming directed at tribal elders. Says Leonard Burch, chairman of the Southern Ute tribe, "More elder programming is needed from the station. This group is often overlooked, and programming in the language that centers on issues relevant to this group would provide better service."[39]

The president of the Ramah Navajo tribe concurs with Burch, adding, "Elders are often neglected, and this is regrettable. However, I realize funds are limited at the station, so this cuts into the amount of elder-oriented programming the station is capable of offering."[40]

Although listeners to Native stations seem uniformly enthusiastic about the amount of information programming they get, there are still those who feel that more is needed. For instance, a survey conducted by KIDE in 1993 revealed that the majority of its audience was not satisfied with the levels of news and information the station aired, especially as pertains to other tribes and on other reservations throughout the country.

Reflecting back at the incident at KILI wherein a staff person was relieved of her on-air duties for using her program to proselytize about her political point of view, Mike Her Many Horses believes that Native stations have to be more conscientious in their efforts to offer balanced broadcasts. "There's some libelous stuff going over the airwaves at times. More responsible programming is needed. Stations shouldn't be exploited for personal gain. They are there to serve everyone."[41]

Conversely, programming is often perceived as too frivolous, says Michael Jandreau, chair of the Lower Brule Sioux. "Substance is often lacking. There's not enough serious programming. There's too much pandering to the superficial tastes of the audience rather than serious attempts at elevating it. Native stations need to build bridges more than entertain. Too often they sound like Anglo stations."[42]

In the opinion of Rose Robinson of the National Congress of American Indians, broadcasting in general seldom delves as deeply as the press. "Regardless of whether they're Anglo or Native stations, they tend to focus on the instant fix but give little information beyond the basics. Indigenous people, like most, get their details from the newspaper."[43]

Carole Standing Elk, who heads the California chapter of AIM, believes that many Indigenous stations start out with noble aspirations but then lapse into complacency. "Many Native radio stations begin with progressive and ambitious agendas but turn conservative. Their potential for real good goes unrealized."[44]

While Ray Cook concurs with Standing Elk on this point, he adds that First Amendment rights as enjoyed by mainstream broadcasters typically do not exist in Native electronic media because federal Indian law does not promote freedom of speech. Therefore there exist constraints that do not inspire such things as in-depth news reporting and investigative journalism.

Inadequate announcer skills are commonly cited as a weakness in Native broadcasts. The following response in a station survey reveals one listener's level of frustration: "Your announcer can't speak clearly. You need to get someone better. Someone who is good in using the language—both Navajo and English. You will lose your audience if you don't get someone who people can understand."[45]

Listener dissatisfaction with Native stations also stems from displeasure with the type of music aired. According to a study by Eiselein, stations KEYA, WOJB, KNNB, KABR, KSHI, and KSUT were criticized for their music programming. [46]

On this point, WOJB's Camille Lacapa-Morrison observes:

Our signal extends to five other Ojibwe reservations besides Lac Court Oreilles. A potential of 8,000 Indian people tune in at least once a week. The biggest complaint I hear from the Native community is that we don't play enough country music. Our station is very unique because we play everything. I've heard non-Native people comment that we should play Indian music twenty-four hours a day because we're an Indian station. My response to that is "Indian people enjoy the same things that you do."[47]

As with most public radio station listeners, Native listeners are sometimes irritated with on-air fund-raising efforts. "Sometimes I think that too much time is spent on trying to raise money, but I realize that these broadcasts are necessary to keep the station going,"[48] comments Mike Her Many Horses.

Listener dissatisfaction with Indigenous stations certainly contributes to the fact that in areas served by mainstream broadcast services Native stations often find themselves secondary radio sources.[49]

On a final note, Joseph Orozco suggests that criticism of Native stations may need to be examined from the perspective of the entitlement mentality of tribal people as created by the BIA/federal entitlement economies. He asks, "Has this created the expectation that every listener is entitled to exactly what he or she wants from the radio station? What does this do to perceptions of station performance?"[50]

## NATIVE STATIONS AND THE MAINSTREAM
## COMMUNITY

Native stations and programs make a contribution to mainstream society by demystifying Indian culture and enhancing Anglo awareness of the value and worth of Indigenous people.

Says AIM's Vernon Bellecourt, "The non-Indian is seldom educated about Indigenous contributions to mass society. Native media can change this. When it does this, it is making an important contribution to the lives of everyone."[51]

Michael Goldberg, coordinator of the Superior Radio Network, offers his non-Indian perspective on the value of Native broadcasting: "To me the key thing about Native radio is the degree to which it enables me and my white neighbors to hear the voices and understand the interests of our Native neighbors. It is then that we begin to acknowledge the truth about white racism and begin to heal ourselves."[52]

Native radio can reduce racial animosity and prejudice between Indians and whites, observes Nan Rubin: "Stations can play an important role in reducing tension. [Native] radio is an intimate, powerful way to reach people, and they respond to it in a very personal way. If any of the reservation-based stations choose to make this one of their priorities, they could have a long-term impact on improving community relations within their regions."[53]

This service by Native stations will ultimately enrich all of American society, contends Eiselein.

There is a need to teach non-Indians about the Indian's heritage and the Indian today about being American. All of the issues we have discussed are issues because they are points of conflict between the Euroamerican society and the many Indian cultures. The creation of solutions requires that non-Indians understand these issues through Indian eyes.

There is a need to teach non-Indians to celebrate a diversity of cultures as a national treasure and a source of strength for dealing with future challenges. We can no longer afford to have people—both Indians and non-Indians—wallow in the narrow ignorance of the false promises of racial superiority.[54]

Adds Eiselein, "Native radio can be a culture broker. It can help bridge the distance between two cultures by teaching the value of one to the other."[55]

Some Native stations direct programming to non-Indian listeners. Powerful KTNN on the Navajo nation airs a program called *Navajo Nights,* which is designed for the station's non-Native listeners. The following statement was excerpted from a station promotional piece.

*Navajo Nights* offers an opportunity to provide the non-Indian [with] public information in such areas as Indian Music—it doesn't all sound the same, and Indian People—they aren't all just one big tribe but many different tribes with many different lifestyles, needs and contributions. *Navajo Nights* will present information through its link with *National Native News*; it will present entertainment via Native American music and interviews with the musicians who make the sounds of Native America, whether it's traditional or contemporary. It will offer stimulation by teaching and relating the Indian experience so that listeners may understand the similarities and differences between the Navajo, other Native Americans, and non-Indians in this country.[56]

Native stations have received kudos from various quarters of mainstream media as well as from state governments for their service to the non-Indian audience. Father Gill of KINI provides the following exerpts from letters that typify the sentiments expressed by many non-Indians for his station's broadcasts.

Over the last few months I've frequently crossed South Dakota on I–90 and this has given me the opportunity to hear your station. I just wanted to let you and your staff know how much I enjoy your station. KINI is doing a great service to the community with your frequent community announcements, news, science features, and non-stop good music. I like the request show and love the native Lakota music. Your people obviously care greatly for the listening audience. I want you to know my respect and admiration for the courage on KINI. We share the vision that through the sky we can communicate ideas that will make life better.[57]

I have enjoyed your programming when I have been on assignment in your part of the country. Despite the rise of television and cable and satellites, radio remains an extremely important medium of communications. It's still the fastest way to disseminate information. And it is my firm belief that radio stations serving Native Americans perform a vital and crucial function.[58]

I want to take this opportunity to thank KINI for airing the AIDS public-service announcements we provided your station. Education is our best weapon against the disease and the media have played an important role in this effort, through both news stories and public service announcements. We appreciate your generous contribution to that effort here in South Dakota.[59]

On the national level, Native programs aired by the public networks have enhanced mainstream society's understanding and appreciation of the concerns and interests that exist in Indian country.

*Chapter Six*

# Traversing the Gorge: Challenges for Indian Broadcasters

███

> In my vision the electric light will stop sometime. It is used too much for TV and going to the moon.
>
> —Lame Deer, Oglala medicine man

## LACK OF MONEY

As part of this study, a questionnaire was distributed to managers of all known Native stations to ascertain the most significant problems and challenges confronting them. Twenty-one managers responded.

Shortage of funds topped their concern list. Given the comments in chapter 3, this problem comes as no surprise. Lack of funding is a universal dilemma in public broadcasting and in particular in the Native sector.

Many Native stations are paying off construction and equipment loans, including those which enjoy relative prosperity compared to their broadcast brethren. "At the moment, CKON's undergoing a debt recovery program. It has taken quite a length of time to do this. Our first priority is to eliminate the station's outstanding debts. As you'd imagine, this is an uphill climb,"[1] says general manager Kallen M. Martin.

Funding for the barest necessities is sometimes next to impossible, observes KMHA's Pete Coffey. "Money to keep things going has been a problem in the past and it continues to be. It will probably always be a struggle to keep the utility bills paid and the lights burning at Native stations."[2]

To most Native managers, money is viewed as the panacea for the ills plaguing their stations. "I'd say that adequate funding would solve all of our existing problems at KSKO, and this is probably the case at other stations like ours. This may seem like an oversimplified cure-all, but the problems that interfere most with operations are money-related,"[3] says former manager Susan Braine.

ICA believes that acute financial deficits are the root cause of many of the difficulties that Native stations face.

The stations suffer from chronic financial shortages due to insufficient on-going financial support. Most stations are staffed by people who come into the system with little or no training, experience or appropriate skills. Training opportunities are limited and station support is often a low priority. A lack of understanding of the business creates additional difficulties. The technical capability is below the industry norm, both in skills and maintenance. A real problem is the cost of conventional broadcast technology. Basically, we are regulated into using high energy absorbing technology and high financing technology in areas of the country where solar and wind energy are high and money is low. In Northern Canada you will find low power short wave radio in use. In the remote mountains of Guatemala in the late 1970's you would find battery powered radio transmitters and receivers in heavy use. The issues and realities of alternative and appropriate technologies seems to have never been considered, which is hard to believe when you realize how many hippie tech-heads found a career in Public Broadcasting. It's like their light bulbs burned out as soon as they hopped on board this train. KU-band satellite technology is the cheapest form of distribution around, even NPR uses it for their news gathering, yet the more expensive C-band system is used. That makes no real sense. On top of the expense of the C-band technology itself are the high D/I fees. It is like the system is locking-out rural and minority voices deliberately. At least, you begin to get that feeling. The bottom line is that finanical stability is a far-fetched dream.[4]

Locating monetary resources to both launch a station and keep it on the air is almost impossible because of the unique conditions present in much of the Native community. According to E. B. Eiselein:

Putting a radio station on the air and keeping it there costs money. This is the first obstacle which reservation radio stations face. As "public" broadcasting in the United States has shifted from the idea of public support through tax dollars in the 1960's to the present policy of listener and corporate underwriting, obtaining finances has become a very different thing. While reservation Native Americans need public radio and the services it provides, the present funding system stacks the deck against tribal stations. Listener support is not a viable method on most reservations. With unemployment over 50 percent on many reservations, it is not surprising that the donor pool is pretty dry. Sending money into your public station is not a priorty when your stomach is empty and the roof is leaking.[5]

Ray Cook believes that Washington funding sources are not in touch with the special conditions that Native stations must operate under compared to those public stations in mainstream environments. "When Native stations are lumped together with everyone else, they are denied. We stand singular in our situations, and that is something that is overlooked to the profound detriment of our medium. DC would like to see us conform to its percep-tions, but that is impossible."[6]

The preceding comments on station funding problems echo views found in chapter 3 and are representative of other comments that cite this specific issue in the study's questionnaire. Nearly all of the various concerns expressed in the questionnaire may be either directly or indirectly attributed to financial deficits as well.

## INADEQUATE STAFFING AND TRAINING

Finding native people to fill station slots is a never ending headache for the majority of Native stations. For some, going off the reservation to find personnel is the only answer. Others even resort to filling positions with non-Indians.

As a consultant to Native stations, Mary Dinota says that while this practice may address the immediate problem of filling the airtime, there are ramifications:

The economic conditions on most reservations have made it extremely difficult for Native owned and operated stations to hire and/or train sufficient staff to produce local programming or to acquire programming to meet community needs. Exam-ining these stations, it appeared to me that one of the major problems Native stations had in operating was the lack of trained *local* Native personnel. Too often it was necessary for licensees to bring in non-Natives to operate their stations. Outsiders, not knowing the local culture, were not able to adequately respond to local needs, and this caused discord at some locations. Over the years, the Corporation for Public Broadcasting has sponsored training events which have helped somewhat. More and more, skilled Native managers will emerge as trained station personnel gain experience in the complex business of operating a public radio station. Until Native people are in key positions at their stations, the intent of Congress has not been fulfilled and conflict with reservation leaders can be expected to continue.[7]

In most cases Native stations are the training ground for the personnel who ultimately staff them, because there are few Native Americans with formal broadcast training. "Where are they going to get it? There aren't many Natives educated in the practices of radio, so there's virtually no pool of qualified applicants for stations to draw from,"[8] says Eiselein.

KBRW's Don Rinker agrees, "You can't go out and hire a trained [Indian] staff. It isn't out there, and there's a lack of qualified management people too, so this places the burden on the station to do it all."[9]

Channel 56's Janet Sauer also laments the absence of qualified personnel. "Here we draw on students to prepare the programming, but first we must train them in what to do. While this is very gratifying, it certainly adds additional demands and pressures on management. But there's really no alternative. Out here there is a dramatic lack of trained [Native] people. That is a simple fact, so if you want to broadcast to the people, you do what you've got to do."[10]

Staffing and training is no less a problem in Alaska than it is in the continental United States, notes KOTZ's former manager, Bob Rawls. "Finding qualified Alaska Natives to fill key positions is a real task, so we're constantly having to train people in broadcast operations. That makes us an educational establishment as well as a station. Unlike most mainstreamers, we face a double responsibility."[11]

Even when trainees are available, the job of educating them in the methods of broadcasting is often an arduous experience. "Radio is a pretty specialized profession, so it's not something you can teach people overnight. You have to invest of your time and expertise to get people where they need to be in order for them to be of real value to you,"[12] says KTDB's Barbara Maria.

Compounding the recruitment problem is the reluctance of some males to become involved in what they perceive as "female" work. Says KIYU's Bob Sommer, "Recruiting Natives to broadcasting is our biggest problem. It's almost impossible to recruit a Native male. They look at radio as 'indoor work' and 'unmanly.' They are the hunters and providers, and as such they must work hard at an outdoor job."[13]

Sommer's statement is born out by the fact that at many Native stations the number of female employees significantly outnumbers male employees. For example, in the early days of KSUT, its entire regular staff was comprised of females.[14]

A reluctance to become involved with broadcasting exists in many Native Americans, and the reason does not always stem from gender role issues. "There's a hesitation by many Natives to perform on the air. This comes from a fear of being criticized or ostracized by tribal members. This isn't so much from a lack of self-esteem but rather a desire to avoid creating jealousies amongst peers. There's lots of intertribal problems that inhibit people from station involvement,"[15] contends KWSO's Michael Villalobos.

Better ways to recruit staff for Native stations need to be devised, according to KNNB's Phoebe Nez. "We've just got to find or develop a better system for recruiting station personnel. Finding volunteers interested in broadcasting is not always easy. That's the first step."[16]

According to Nan Rubin, finding station volunteers on reservations is complicated by discouraging conditions:

There are few Native Americans trained in management skills willing to work at these radio stations. Most of the station managers were ill-prepared for this specialized position and have had to learn their skills on-the-job. Tribal members trained in such station needs as production and development are rare. Training opportunities for staff are limited, and the relative isolation of these stations makes it difficult to participate in public radio training activities. Volunteers come to the station unskilled, and their ability to become trained rests solely with the level of skill already existing at the station.

The same isolation and unfamiliar cultural context do not attract many non-Indians to become staff at reservation stations. There is some ambivalence at the stations about having non-Indian staff members.

The cultural background of many Indian people does not include the concept of "volunteering." In areas with such high unemployment, the idea of working for nothing runs counter to the need to find paying work.

Because the different communities on many reservations are widely separated, traveling between them is often difficult. The long distance, severe weather, and lack of reliable transportation keep the number of available volunteers low.[17]

To compound difficulties even further, retaining station personnel is difficult, especially in areas where other opportunities exist. Some Alaska stations have experienced particularly high rates of employee turnover, owing to the fact that better-paying industries exist close by.

## LACK OF NATIVE-LANGUAGE SKILLS

Native station managers find that many of the young people they recruit have been overassimilated into mainstream culture, a condition that has left them ignorant of tribal traditions and language. "I can't recount the number of times we've hired a Native only to find out later that he or she can't speak their own language,"[18] says Barbara Maria.

When that happens, these individuals are unable to assist in Native-language programs or those that contain traditional themes, and this inability means that a station's efforts in these areas may be significantly compromised. If a station's staff is lacking an adequate knowledge of the culture the facility is intended to serve, then it is not really serving anybody, contends Eiselein. "A station staff has to have cultural skills if the station is to live up to its expectations and the expectations of those people relying on it across the reservation. The problem is that too many of those who are broadcasting out there are more culturally Anglo than they are Indian."[19]

When Stu Schader took over as manager of KGHR, a station largely staffed by students, he discovered that English was the only language spoken by the overwhelming majority of those who worked on the air. Disturbed by this situation, Schader implemented efforts to bring the language back to the station and its staff.

One problem that we've confronted is the lack of young Navajos and Hopis who are able to speak their Native language. Obviously there is a need to keep these languages alive as a way to help preserve the traditions and culture of these people. During the 1992–1993 school year, I initiated a broadcast seminar featuring broadcasters from around the state. Among the invited guests was Selina Many-Children from KTNN in Window Rock. Selina is a role model for all Native American broadcasters because of her ability to communicate bilingually in English and Navajo in an instant. The students look up to her and recognize her importance and impact on reservation inhabitants. She emphasized the need for multi-language speaking as a means for communicating over the air and as a way to keep Native American traditions and customs alive. The students responded positively by producing announcements in Navajo for KGHR. Now we're trying as best we can to integrate Native language into our regular schedule of programs.[20]

Although more and more, Native stations would like to require that staff people, in particular on-air personnel, have bilingual speaking skills, the shortage of available staff in many locations means that expectations have to be adjusted downward.

## POOR FACILITIES AND EQUIPMENT

The obvious consequence of funding shortages is substandard facilities and equipment. Nearly all of those station managers surveyed for this book cited decrepit physical plants as a major problem. "Unfortunately in Native broadcasting the facilities that house the stations are often objects of a bygone era. Call them archives. They could justifiably be described as relics of the past, because by no stretch of the imagination do they reflect the changing times. They're barely in sync with the lowest echelon of stations in the country. Antiquated is the best word."[21]

Deficiencies in this area affect the quality of service that Native stations wish to offer their listeners. When you don't have what you need to be a full-service operation, people suffer, says KCUK's Peter Tuluk. "The biggest problem confronting our station is inadequate equipment or the absence of necessary gear to reach the listening audience in the other two communities KCUK is licensed to serve. So they go without, and this really adds to everyone's frustration."[22]

KBRW's Don Rinker expresses similar dissatisfaction with the state of equipment in Native radio. "It's too bad given what these stations are trying to accomplish that they have to contend with such poor facilities. It's a case of trying to do so much with so little."[23]

Not only do many Native stations work with inferior apparatus, but some lack the capability even to take advantage of available outside programming services that could be offered to their listeners. According to Mary Dinota:

Up until recently, Native programming was not available to Native stations, and now that it is, some cannot even take advantage of it because they do not have sufficient receiver equipment to utilize the national feed. It all comes down to inadequate operating budgets. Not all stations have been able to raise sufficient local operating funds to become qualified for a community service grant from CPB. Community licensed stations have a particularly difficult time. Those licensed to institutions, i.e., school districts or colleges, with an ongoing fiscal base were usually on more sound footing, inasmuch as they were housed at the institution and did not have to pay rent or electricity. Native controlled community stations are not so lucky.[24]

Given the unfavorable economic situation that exists at most stations, it is unlikely that the equipment problem will vanish any time soon. Although there are noteworthy exceptions, many (if not the majority) of Native stations will continue to work with physical plants that resemble broadcast museum exhibits rather than state-of-the-art facilities.

## TRIBAL INTERFERENCE

The question of station governance is a prominent issue, especially when a facility is licensed to a tribe. Stations wish to operate with a measure of autonomy, which they feel is necessary in order to perform effectively as a mass medium, but tribal councils and boards sometimes impose strictures that make independence difficult.

Tribal interference in station operations has many managers at a boiling point. Hostilities run high at Native stations because nonbroadcasters are encroaching in areas where they don't belong, according to KMHA's Pete Coffey.

As a ten-year veteran of radio, not just Indian radio, the biggest issue I see is tribal governments dictating or attempting to dictate station policy and practice to those who know radio and have been trained to act impartially in the preparation and reporting of tribal news—whether good or bad. Native radio should be removed from under the tribal government umbrella as a way to remedy this problem. Many station managers and senior station staff have been removed or replaced when a new council regime comes into office with its own agenda. I've seen three station managers removed during my tenure as director of programs, operations, and public affairs. The local tribal government has this control since they are the body which appoints the station's board of directors. At least that's the case here. Maybe the application of the Indian Civil Rights Act would help, but those of us who must work under the tribal government's auspices know there are no civil rights on reservations. Those Indian people working in outside media tell us how to report the news, despite the pressure we're under here. Obviously they have never worked on a reservation or under tribal rule. It's fine for them to champion the First Amendment, but will they pay our bills or provide us with food and clothing for our children if we do report the news the way it should be reported and find ourselves unemployed?[25]

E. B. Eiselein is sympathetic to Coffey's perspective, adding, "Tribal leaders can be a real barrier to Native stations. I found that many tribal leaders don't really understand what tribal radio is all about and its potential for serving tribal members."[26]

Regrettably, too many tribal leaders want to use stations for political means, says Phoebe Nez. "When a Native station is owned and operated by the tribe, the tribal leaders tend to start managing the station when things don't satisfy their views. A station should be a place where a variety of political views are expressed, but when tribal leaders have a specific political program they want the station to be their exclusive pulpit."[27]

When stations are licensed to elected tribal boards, it is almost inevitable that they become ensnared in the political machinations, says Nan Rubin:

Tribal politics are often volatile and council elections are often highly emotional. Too frequently the radio stations are subject to being used for political ends, and their ability to secure tribal support may depend more on staying in favor with the current leadership than on their public radio activities. This keeps the station in a state of insecurity and powerlessness.

A major ongoing problem that station staff are unable to address on their own is the unstable nature of their own governing boards and the unpredictable impact that the boards exercise.[28]

This situation has historical roots, observes ICA's Ray Cook.

Native radio needs to address the impact made by the forced relocation and assimilationist policies of the 1920's, 1930's, and 1940's. The long-term effects of these oppressive U.S. policies have resulted in Native communities having inherited oppression syndrome. This affliction causes major disruptions in the local socio-economic system, which in turn affects a station's ability to execute good decisions. The CPB funded "ICA Governance Project" seeks to strengthen the fragile governance of Native radio. We hope to provide a way of obtaining effective understanding, long-term security and operational autonomy for Native stations. Because the governance of most Native radio stations is closely tied to the politics of their tribal governments, and because most Native communities are still reeling from the effects of forcibly imposed governance systems, stations often find themselves in situations which are problematic, contentious, and demoralizing, much like the Jewish councils of the Polish ghettos during Nazi reign.[29]

Tribal interference in station operations is not always politically inspired. Some tribal council or board members want to be program directors, observes KTDB's Barbara Maria. "Problems sometimes occur when tribal governments want to tell stations what they should be playing . . . what songs, what features, and so on. It's very difficult if a station is in this situation. Fortunately for us we're not, and I think that's why we've been successful."[30]

As Maria indicates, not all tribal boards interfere with the operation of the broadcast station for which they hold the license. In fact, some are pretty apathetic about them. "Our council really doesn't become involved in what we do. In fact, it doesn't pay much attention to us at all. Of the council's seven members, I think only two or three actually listen,"[31] notes WOJB's Lacapa-Morrison.

Other pieces of tribal legislation have interrupted the normal tranquility of Native station operations. For example, when KIDE's licensee, the Hoopa tribe, implemented mandatory random drug testing for all station employees, its manager challenged his "safety sensitive" classification, arguing that he was not given proper notification as called for by the tribe's policies. The tribe placed him on indefinite suspension, and litigation continues at this writing. It is not likely that the manager will return to the station.

Instances abound where tribal interference in station activities has inspired controversy. What happened at KILI, where members of the reservation's council wanted to oust the station's acting general manager, is a stellar example. (See chapter 4.)

## LACK OF NATIVE PROGRAMMING

The primary fare at Native stations is music—Anglo music. Country music is more prevalent on most Native stations than any other element of programming. Other forms of mainstream music constitute a large part of the broadcast day, but the amount of traditional and contemporary Native music aired is growing.

Native programming is not abundant because it must come from the efforts of the local stations, which are faced with limitations when it comes to manufacturing air product themselves. There has not been a lot available from national resources, and (as already discussed) having access to it has been a problem. "Nationally produced non-music programming relevant to Indian listeners is virtually non-existent within the public radio system,"[32] reports Nan Rubin.

Stations indicate that they would like to have more Native programs to offer listeners, but obtaining them is difficult. "Finding and acquiring Native Alaskan and Native American programming is a big problem. There never seems enough,"[33] observes Bob Rawls. This is very true, says KBRW's Don Rinker. "There is a real dearth of programming that targets the Native American audience, so stations have to produce their own, and there's only so much you can do."[34]

Ray Cook contends that the lack of local and national Native programming can be directly linked to CPB's Program Fund and other foundations and corporations that fail to grasp the fact that Native nations wish to originate their own programming. Cook holds that these funding entities are intent on allocating resources to urban-based production houses that often are not wholly connected to the Native community. Funders have not helped stations maintain their production plants, so program production remains on the wish list, argues Cook.

Many Native stations feel they are discriminated against by record companies, which often are disinclined to provide them with the kind of service they offer mainstream broadcasters. "KGHR has had some real problems getting music service from the record companies, so we have to go out and purchase music from record stores. Getting programming material requires a major effort, but you get results every so often."[35]

With the advent of the AIROS programming service, which was scheduled to debut in 1994, Native programming availability will be greatly enhanced for those stations equipped to receive it.

## COMPETITION

In their reports to CPB on Native radio station listening, both Eiselein and Rubin have found that many of these stations share mainstream station concern about competition from other broadcast sources.

In fact, while many Native stations are the dominant listening sources in their areas, a number do not do as well as Anglo stations in garnering Indian listeners. KGHR's Stu Schader is cognizant of this fact in his particular market.

Although Native American radio stations have the biggest lifestyle connection to those living on the Navajo reservation, they are not listened to exclusively or even primarily. Native Americans listen to a variety of off-reservation commercial radio stations. Local businesses targeting Navajos advertise on off-reservation stations because they know they [Navajos] are tuned into these non-Indian stations. The businesses on the reservation will listen to off-reservation stations, too, to keep up on things. Certainly there is a sense of loyalty for the Native station for a variety of reasons, but by no means is the Native American station listened to primarily.[36]

KSHI's Duane Chimoni says that many Native listeners go elsewhere for the sake of variety and a basic interest in mainstream culture or for programming they regard as more relevant to their needs.

Mostly, Indians here tune the station, but I think in general they approach listening like anyone else. Sometimes the programming on Native stations just doesn't make sense to them; they don't understand it. The concept of "community" or "public" radio is not always embraced by Native listeners, just as it is not always embraced by whites. Programming that does not "mean" something is often turned off for a more entertaining format, which usually is provided by the local commercial stations.[37]

The FCC's Allen Myers speculates that some Native stations contribute to audience tuneout because they are unclear as to just whom they're targeting for an audience. "A real problem at times for these stations is figuring whom they're going to serve. They know they're out there to serve, but whom exactly are they serving?"[38]

On this last point, several Native stations have become more involved with researching their signal areas as a means of gaining a clearer grasp of their potential audience and what it wants.

## OTHER CONCERNS

The preceding concerns of Native station managers constitute the most prominent of those cited in the study's questionnaire, but other issues were mentioned.

Racism by non-Indians was indicated as a problem, particularly when it came to station fund-raising campaigns, because these efforts were sometimes construed as competitive by Anglo businesses.

Another area of concern for some station managers and program directors was the inability to get programs produced, even when funds were available, because the right people were not available.

KSHI's Chimoni observes that there is much Native stations need to do but often cannot do.

Native stations need to focus on alleviating some of the major problems in the community, such as alcoholism, child-spouse-elderly abuse, apathy, low Native pride. There's a lot of talk on these subjects, but not a lot of programs. They need to be produced by Indigenous people, who have experienced these bad times. Getting these people in to assist with making these programs has not been done enough because it's not easy.[39]

In another area, Native managers expressed the belief that finding employees is often hampered by the fact that the broadcast field is viewed as a deadend by Indians because so few opportunities exist for them outside the local station.

The National Association of Broadcasters's Dwight Ellis confirms the perception by would-be Native broadcasters that the field is not exactly fertile ground for them:

Current employment trends reported by the FCC reveal very little growth between 1980 and 1992 in Native American broadcast employment. The percentage of Native American full-time employees was .5 percent from 1980 to 1989. From 1990 to 1992, there was only a .1 percent increase in employment. While other minorities and white females have shown gradual increases, the pattern of Native American employment has been disappointing.[40]

Finally, a concern indicated by several Native managers centered around the lack of connectedness between stations. Although these stations considered themselves to be a part of the same unique club, there was little sense of unity or link between individual stations. Most of the managers citing this as a problem also indicated that with the launch of AIROS and the continued work of ICA, this situation would change.

Despite the multitude of problems Native station managers say they must contend with, they are uniform in their belief that what they are doing is a good and noble thing, and almost all indicate they would not want to be doing something else.

NFCB president Lynn Chadwick applauds the efforts and dedication of the staff and managers who keep the Native signals in the air.

In joining together, the Native stations have had to compromise and learn about each other's needs and perspectives, setting aside cultural and political differences from past generations. The road has been hard. They have learned a great deal. Public broadcasters and many others could learn much from the experiences of the dedicated people who have built and maintained these stations.[41]

## CHALLENGES

ICA's Joseph Orozco contributes a concluding word on the challenges of traversing the gorge.

When one asks a Native radio station manager what major problem the medium faces, he or she often says financial instability. To those embroiled in day-to-day operations, technical training, the retention of quality staff, equipment purchasing, and staff shortages may also come to mind.

However, I think such issues are only symptoms of a larger, ongoing problem. The major problem facing Native radio is the same that faces Native newspapers—inherited oppression. Our own tribal governments, our own tribal people, are the major barriers to the free exercise of the First Amendment by Native media.

Over the generations, Native people have learned not to trust one another. We have learned that it is possible to bully others to go along with us. One of the great fallacies we continue to perpetuate, usually at the tribal council level, is the notion that if we keep control of the amount and type of information that goes out, we can maintain control and protection of our destiny. Whether we are ready or not, we are in the information age. The world is now based on the free flow of information. Those who horde this resource for themselves will find themselves alone or in very sparse company. The people deserve and demand to know all truths, and they will find means by which to gain access to them.

Looking at what has happened to our people historically shows that what happened was not our ancestors' choice. However, it is our people's responsibility to stop oppressing one another today. Many of our tribes have gone through lengthy court battles for land, resources, and subsistence rights, and they have been involved in legislative actions and a myriad of other important issues.

Tribal councils took measures to silence journalistic news media coverage as a way to feel secure. In the 1970s we experienced a need for secrecy as tribal departments competed for federal funds against their counterparts from other tribes. These actions were considered as important as the CIA's classification of "National Security." Such actions emphasized the need to maintain control over all tribal entities. When radio came to the "rez," it was scooped into the same net. If it is a tribal entity, then tribal people must maintain control. Does this mean all tribal people? Or does it mean just those tribal people who convinced others of the need to take control?

Another look at our past shows that every tribe honored the right for every person to have a say. This tradition may have meant that people have the right to speak their minds without interference. It did not mean that those who spoke the loudest or the harshest got their way, as is often the case today. It meant that everyone had the right to tell his or her version of reality. After all had spoken, a decision was made based upon what had been heard. More details were considered than this simple example suggests. In relation to the purpose of radio on the reservation, one can liken its function to that of the Talking Stick, the Talking Circle, or even the mediator or the go-between.

People need radio and newspapers to learn as many versions of reality as they can. People need access to radio and newspapers to tell their stories and share their insights. Some tribal governments and some tribal people bar some people from access to radio or newspapers for fear of what they could say or might say. There are healthy tribal governments that do support the media and the exchange of ideas. Perhaps more tribal councils will follow their example. As the American statesman, Adlai Stevenson once said, "The greatness of a government can be measured by the extent to which it invites and encourages public scrutiny."

## Chapter Seven

# In the Hands of Oyaron: Prospects for Native Broadcasting

Yesterday and tomorrow exist eternally upon this continent.
— Peter Blue Cloud, Mohawk

## THE PATH AHEAD

The future for Native broadcasting seems at once both bright and uncertain. While some stations will no doubt continue to battle the specter of insolvency, many will find the path less toilsome and their hopes more fully realized.

Several things will play a role in Native broadcasting's future. Technology is one. A satellite will beam Indian programs to an expanding number of Native stations and the world, while the audio medium's ultimate move to the digital domain may pose both additional obstacles and opportunities for Indigenous broadcasters.

In 1994 AIROS was scheduled to provide Native stations with a unique programming service. It is hard to overstate the significance of this new audio distribution system, says broadcast engineer Alex Looking Elk. "With the AIROS satellite downloading programming to stations, there finally is a means of connection between Native outlets. This linkage strengthens the medium on a number of significant levels. In many respects, it is the key to the future of Native broadcasting."[1]

Oyaron is the spirit being to the Iroquois who controls destiny.

KGHR's Stu Schader concurs with Looking Elk. "In my opinion, the future of Native broadcasting is directly tied to AIROS. It will greatly enhance the quality of programming Indigenous stations offer their listeners, which in turn will make them more competitive and viable."[2]

Other new and evolving broadcast technologies may play a key role in the future of Native radio and television. As of this writing, however these innovations have yet to appear in the mainstream, although their arrival appears inevitable.

One of these innovations is digital audio broadcasting, known simply as DAB. As the world converts from analog to digital sound reproduction, the radio medium believes that it must do likewise in order to remain an appealing option for music listeners. Despite the preponderance of news and talk programming on radio, music remains the foremost reason people tune in.

Although DAB promises to give radio CD-quality sound, it will require that stations convert their audio processing chain and transmission systems to digital sound. While digital signaling will save stations money in the long run, because it requires less power to transmit, the cost of the switch over to this new modus operandi will not be inexpensive. "When DAB comes about, it will present Native broadcasters with yet another economic concern. But Indian radio has a better chance of survival than Indian video services, because the cost of audio equipment is considerably less. Television is going high definition, and that is cost-intensive,"[3] notes Looking Elk.

Computers are playing an increasing role in Native broadcasting and in the Indigenous community at large. "On more and more reservations, computer technology is recording and teaching native languages, tribal history, and traditional culture and knowledge as well as disseminating current events and information."[4]

While digital audio workstations, which employ computer technology, are the new production tool of choice at more than a quarter of the country's mainstream radio stations, they have yet to appear in equal proportion at Native stations. As prices come down, however, this will change since workstations significantly enhance the usability and potential of the audio production facility.

On the nontechnical front, many Native broadcasters are wondering whether the profits generated by Indian gaming throughout the country will aid their particular cause. Today Native gaming (what some non-Indians sceptically refer to as the "Indian's revenge") is a multibillion-dollar industry and growing. Several dozen Native gambling establishments are in operation, or about to begin operation, throughout the country.

The questions many are contemplating are whether or not all tribes will be in on the prosperity, even those without casinos, and whether or not the wealth will be spread around to the extent that it will reach Native stations.

For many Natives the idea of appealing to fellow Natives for underwriting funds is much more palatable than going to CPB or other predominantly non-Indian sources. The bottom line may be how effective Native stations are at arguing for support, that is, assuming the gaming industry has altruistic interests that include Indigenous broadcasting. Says Charles Trimble, "If stations can make a case for monies, they may benefit from gaming receipts, but there may be a long line."[5]

Working to enhance this prospect is the Indian Gaming Regulatory Act, which provides that not more than 20 percent of gaming hall revenues can go to per capita payments, so 80 percent goes into tribal discretionary funds, which includes money for development.

Fanning Native public broadcasters' hopes of benefiting from the success of Indian gaming is the view of Rick Hill, chairman of the National Indian Gaming Association, who holds that gaming "is the catalyst tribes need to build healthy economies, create jobs and improve human services on reservations while decreasing tribal dependence on federal and state tax dollars."[6]

Tribes that have gaming investments and possess station licenses are the likeliest to allocate more funds, says Trimble. "To the extent a tribe is the licensee of a station and involved in gaming, it may earmark some additional support monies."[7]

Such was the case with Florida's Seminole tribe, which earmarked some of its bingo earnings for the acquisition of video equipment for use over its cable channel, WSBC. The tribe has expressed hopes of acquiring a regular television station if it is able to build a proposed casino. In May 1994 the tribe was awaiting approval to build a gaming complex.

It is not unrealistic to assume that tribes with burgeoning pocketbooks from gaming profits will seek to expand their investment portfolios by acquiring mainstream broadcast stations, which they would doubtless continue to operate as revenue generators. If this occurs, it is difficult to predict whether or not it would benefit Native broadcasters by enhancing their employment prospects at these Indian-owned stations. Certainly the overall employment situation has improved for Natives where Indian gaming facilities operate.

At this writing, the question as to what extent, if any, the expanding economic base created by Indian gaming will benefit Native broadcasting is a difficult one to answer. It would seem, however, that the upturn in Indigenous economic fortunes resulting from the rapid growth of this industry can only increase the optimism of Native broadcasters, whose funding prospects have hitherto been so circumscribed.

With or without support from the gaming industry, Native broadcasters foresee improved conditions at stations. "I think we're all going to become much more self-sufficient in the future. With our own satellite programming service and station support organization, things are headed in a positive direction,"[8] says KNNB's Phoebe Nez, whose opinion is shared by fellow Native broadcaster Pete Coffey. "I envision a strong and independent Indian broadcast industry able to more effectively address Indigenous issues and concerns."[9]

KCUK's Peter Tuluk expects things to get better all around. "I see a lot of improvements in Native programming and greater support from state government, especially here in Alaska. You know, I think things are going to get a lot better too for Native people who want careers in broadcasting. There are a growing number of opportunities for Indians, and I expect this to continue in the next few years."[10]

Better Native station service to communities is predicted. "It takes time to develop programming that really means something to the lives of listeners, but that's happening here with an emphasis on education. At the same time, I think communities with Native stations are waking up to their unique value,"[11] observes KIYU's Bob Sommer.

Radio will become an even more integral part of the community, believes KSHI's Duane Chimoni. "It's been slow to dawn on folks out there that this medium can be a very powerful instrument for needed change and improvement in lifestyles. If used properly, a station can be a very valuable resource for a community, and I think people are recognizing that fact."[12]

As Native stations become stronger, they will serve their audiences more effectively, contends KTDB's Barbara Maria. "I see Native stations with modern equipment providing listeners with even more information programming and faster too. Services like language programming will become more prevalent as stations evolve and gain greater stability."[13]

## INTERCONNECTEDNESS

If any one thing will characterize and define Native broadcasting in the future, it is likely to be its interconnectedness. As Alex Looking Elk noted in an earlier section, the AIROS satellite is the future of Native radio.

The concept of a Native satellite programming service is not new. The idea goes back to the late 1970s and early 1980s when NAPBC suggested the creation of an American Indian radio satellite network. As it turned out, this suggestion led to American Indian Radio on Satellite.

It was spearheaded by NAPBC executive director Frank Blythe and ICA executive director Ray Cook. They, along with Joseph Orozco and Bernie Bustos, developed the AIROS mission statement and funding proposal. The project came to fruition in 1992, when CPB allocated funding to the NAPBC for the purpose of developing the AIROS concept.

The argument for AIROS was based in part on the need to eliminate barriers that made it difficult for independent Native and station-based producers to reach a national audience with their unique messages. In addition, the AIROS proposal sought to increase the audience for public radio while providing programming that enlightened as well as entertained.

The proposal foresaw three ways that audience size would be increased through the use of a satellite service:

1. Larger audiences would result with the general improvement and variety of Native station product.

2. Increased listener loyalty would subsequently occur as a result of enhanced programming.

3. Incentive would be created for Native communities to seek their own station, thereby increasing the number of Indigenous broadcast signals.

Audience diversity would also be positively affected by AIROS. "The development of an AIROS network will increase audience diversity in two ways: 1. By expanding the number of Native Americans listening to public radio, and 2. [by] increasing the opportunity for non-Native American listeners of Native stations to hear programs reflecting Indigenous voices, cultures, and issues."[14]

In addition, program sharing among Native stations would be made possible by AIROS, which in turn would make a wealth of material available for general distribution to public radio audiences. "By providing a 24 hour satellite distribution capability for this programming, AIROS will significantly add to the body of illuminating and inspiring programming currently available to national public radio audiences."[15]

The AIROS proposal also cited improved services to Indigenous communities as an inducement for CPB to fund the project. "Satellite distribution will enhance the dissemination of information, such as pertains to education, health, and national policy issues, which are critical to Native American communities."[16]

Uniting the country's Indian communities is the principal goal behind AIROS, says Ray Cook. "The satellite will deliver programs from all areas of Indian Country for the purpose of de-isolating these communities from each other. It will lead to a cohesive national voice for Native Americans. This is an awesome time for Native radio. Milestones like this one are very satisfying, and will help make our goal of bringing radio service to 250 more Native communities by the year 2013 possible."[17]

Based on the NAPBC/ICA proposal, in 1993 CPB provided $460,000 in start-up monies to put the first ever Indian broadcast service on satellite. CPB also allocated an additional $370,000 for AIROS programming in 1994–1995. The National Federation of Community Broadcasters lent down-link technical support, and Michael Goldberg of Superior Radio and Molly Romero and Charles Trimble of Charles Trimble Company contributed a business plan as the project began to move toward fruition.

As of this writing, AIROS, which subleases space on NPR's transponder, was scheduled to begin feeding affiliates programming five days a week in the latter part of the fall of 1994 (the service was to be launched May 30, 1994, but it found itself short of sufficient programming material). It plans to increase daily feeds to six hours by mid-1995. Programming will include an interactive show titled *Native America Calling,* American Indian news segments, features by noted Native producers (*Indigenous Voices*), Native music, and much more.

Over half of the country's Native stations were signed on as members when AIROS premiered, and the remainder were expected to be connected with the satellite programming service within a year. Affiliates pay an annual fee, which is based on their cash budgets. Fees typically begin at $3,500 (a figure still being reviewed at this writing) per year.

Susan Braine, formerly of KSKO, is system manager for AIROS, which is presently headquartered with NAPBC in Lincoln, Nebraska. She warns that the success of the service is in the hands of the individual stations, as well as those of the American public.

AIROS has great potential, especially for the Native owned and operated community radio stations in the United States. The success of this Native content programming service greatly lies with the stations themselves and their ability to produce and share programs with each other and the listening public at large. AIROS' success also depends on whether or not America realizes the importance of assuring that the Native American voice is heard. This means receiving an adequate share of the public broadcasting funding, as well as the mainstream paying heed to the social responsibility of preserving traditional and contemporary Native cultures in this country.[18]

With the information highway and digital technology coming of age, Native communities via AIROS will be able to tell their own stories to the world, says Ray Cook. "We're taking this concept to heart. Not only will we access more information, but our perspectives of world events will be added to the mainstream consciousness. This ought to shift a few old-world paradigms."[19]

The information super highway model of the 1990s has made its way well into Indian country, observes Charles Trimble.

Recently I received a letter from a sharp Indian leader telling me that my work in economic development is important, but that I should pay more attention to the world of high tech, vis-à-vis Indian country. He said that with the new information superhighway coming, the next Indian wars would be fought in cyberspace. My first thought was "Oh, ———, just as we are beginning to win a few battles in our ongoing war for tribal lands and rights, the bastards are now going to change wars on us." Actually, he was right. As someone said, the building of superhighways [has] destroyed many communities and left the members of those communities too poor to enjoy the superhighways. Perhaps Native broadcasters can help build onramps to the new information superhighways for the tribes and help keep our people from being among the road kill.[20]

In the past there have been other attempts to interconnect stations. For example, in their landmark study of Native media *Let My People Know* (p. 143), Jim Murphy and Sharon Murphy note the existence of a regional news network operated by Navajos in the 1970s. While short-lived, it offered daily news and information feeds to stations in the southwest.

Predating the AIROS effort to interconnect Native stations was that of the Superior Radio Network (SRN), which links a handful of stations, both Indian and non-Indian, using land transmission apparatus. Although operated by non-Indians, SRN has a declared mission to serve the needs of the Anishinabe culture. Explains the network's coordinator, Michael Goldberg:

When the four stations in northern Minnesota and northern Wisconsin formed SRN in 1988, there were several considerations that brought us together. The stations themselves are similar in size and orientation (as community access public stations) and all operate in an environment dominated by large centralized state public radio networks. But a more pressing reason for working together was the growing controversy in northern Wisconsin about Native spearfishing rights. This issue was being thoroughly covered by WOJB, licensed by the Lac Court Oreilles Band, and we wanted a mechanism that would allow KAXE and other neighboring stations to inform listeners about the issues related to treaty rights from a Native perspective.

As we discussed our common interests, we agreed that the northern parts of our states have more in common with each other than with the heavily populated southern parts of our states, which dominate the north politically and in terms of media. We identified the region's commonalities in terms of mineral, timber and tourism resources for the economy and agreed that our programming would address the environmental issues common throughout the bio-region. This bio-region is also, and not coincidentally, the traditional and accustomed lands of the Anishinabe people. So we've interconnected our broadcast resources and talents to work toward a common good, the preservation of the natural world. This sense of place is fundamental to Native cultures. We believe that we can improve our understanding of the world and how to live in it by listening to our Native neighbors. That's what this network is about.[21]

Radio services, such as SRN, that produce broadcasts for and about Natives also plan to become involved in the dissemination of their programs via AIROS. At the same time, public networks and station groups (like SRN) are expected to become AIROS member affiliates for its Native programming feeds.

## CONCERNS

The path for Canadian Native broadcasters has been a smooth one compared to the one U.S. Native broadcasters have had to travel, and there are still more potential potholes ahead. Proposed reclassification of Alaska public stations could impose additional hardships on some Indigenous operations there, and threats of massive federal budget cuts in the area of public broadcasting loom darkly. For example, although a budget reduction bill proposed by Colorado's Senator Kerrey and Nebraska's Senator Brown designed to trim back significantly CPB funding was narrowly defeated in the fall of 1993, there were grave concerns that it or another similiar bill would threaten the future of Native broadcasters somewhere down the line.

ICA's Ray Cook sees the fate of AIROS tied to the mood of those who will shape policy in Washington in the months and years ahead.

Based on past events, I'd say AIROS is certainly vulnerable, at least at this point in time. For instance, when CPB was presented with the possibility that the Native broadcast community was considering prioritizing the distribution system first for its own community's purposes (healing, education, resocialization) and [second for] cross-cultural purposes, it threatened to pull back funding unless the issue of cross-culturalism was addressed as priority one. That was very BIA of them. It is not that cross-cultural education is not needed. Indeed, we fully understand the advantages of the occasional, well planned and financed cross-cultural experience (on our terms). The problem is that we are now coerced to abide by [Washington] DC's dictum even when it is not in our perceived best interest to do so. This is something we'll continue to deal with, since we rely on support from outside our own community.[22]

There are those in the Native broadcast community who believe that the future holds a continuation of past problems. Says KBRW's Don Rinker, "Despite AIROS, most stations will stay unconnected in the foreseeable future. Equipment will continue to be substandard and problematic for operators. The pool of programming targeting Natives will not grow substantially, and there will still exist a lack of qualified senior management personnel."[23]

The prospects for growth in the number of Native-owned stations is uncertain, notes the NAB's Dwight Ellis.

Based on recent surveys, Native station ownership growth, especially in television, is rather dismal. This condition must be changed if Native Americans are to have full participation in the information superhighway. Indigenous communities deserve their proper share of communication vehicles for the dissemination of news, information, and entertainment run by people of their own race and culture.[24]

In his January 1994 keynote speech to the Indigenous Communication Association, Charles Trimble cautioned the organization against internal bickering, which could have a deleterious effect on the future of Indian broadcasting. He recounts his own experience with the fledgling American Indian Press Association (AIPA) in this excerpt from his address:

In the late 1960's I was editor of the *Indian Times*, a small newspaper serving the Indian community of Denver. At the time, I was also serving on the board of American Indian Development (AID), a nonprofit organization that sponsored summer workshops in contemporary Indian affairs for college level Indian students. Those were times before many colleges had Indian studies courses.

In 1969, or thereabouts, I was able through AID to secure a small grant to pull together several editors of Indian newspapers to see what we could do to organize ourselves into an association dedicated to improving the lot of Indian newspapers across the country. There were no Indian broadcast media at that time, or none that we were aware of. I remember that we had dreams of someday including Indian radio and television, particularly after Dick LaCourse and I visited the Alberta Native Communications Society in Canada and saw how they had radio and television production and broadcast capability, subsidized by the provincial government. But ours were just dreams.

Although we were never sure at first how many Indian papers were out there, we guessed (maybe inflating our estimates a little) that there were some 100 to 125 publications, ranging in quality from a few pretty slick tabloid-size weeklies to single sheet mimeographed monthlies. Some of the newspapers would exchange complimentary subscriptions, so we had some idea of what other papers were doing and generally what our common problems were. There was no such thing as intellectual property or copyright laws among us, and when there was a good cartoon or editorial or new article you had published, you'd see it in other papers, sometimes months down the line.

At any rate, with the AID grant funds, I called several editors I thought represented a good geographic cross section of Indian country and we decided to get together. The editors included Jim Jefferson of the *Southern Ute Drum*, Mary Baca of the *Jicarilla Chieftain*, Rupert Costo of the *Indian Historian*, Marie Potts of *Smoke Signals* in California, Gwen Owle of the *Cherokee One Feather* in North Carolina, Tom Cook of *Akwesasne Notes*, Carol Wright of the *Native Nevadan*, Tom Conolly of Gonzaga University, and myself [italics added]. It was the first time any of us had ever met in person, and it was a pretty exciting time. At that first meeting, it was pretty well agreed that we should form an association of Indian newspapers, and we decided to seek funds to hold a series of organizational meetings and get other editors involved. In a later meeting we picked up Leo Vocu of the *Lakota Nation News*, Russ Means of the Cleveland Indian Center, Dick LaCourse, who was a reporter with the *Seattle Post-Intelligencer*, and Rose Robinson, who was a reporter with the Bureau of Indian Affairs. Some of us kind of wondered about Rose early on, wondering what the BIA wanted with us. After several meetings around the country, at which we picked up a lot of interest, we finally incorporated in Washington, D.C., in 1971.

The purposes of our new organization were basically to provide a news service, to help improve the technical and editorial quality of the member newspapers, and to provide a network for Indian journalists. Strangely unmentioned in our purposes was that of assuring protection of our collective First Amendment rights. Perhaps this was because of our concern about jeopardizing the tribal support many of the Indian papers depended on, or perhaps it was because we didn't want to appear to be challenging the tribal governments when their existence was threatened by federal policy of "termination." I'm not really sure why we didn't stress First Amendment rights at that time. I'm not sure that it [the First Amendment] holds the priority it deserves among today's Indian media organizations. Regardless, there were plenty of enemies out there to protect our tribes and Indian rights from, and that reoccupied our interests to where we didn't think much about our First Amendment rights under tribal governments.

Indian country reaction to our appearance in Indian affairs was probably best characterized as general indifference. But one tribe saw us as an important addition to Indian affairs. The Colville Tribe was in a death struggle in its final phase of being terminated, and its great leader Lucy Covington asked AIPA to help her put together a newspaper and a propaganda campaign to help defeat the forces of termination. Termination was, of course, the national Indian policy calling for the severance of the federal-tribal trust relationship on a tribe-by-tribe basis, and placing the tribes in the jurisdiction of the states. What I didn't realize was that tribal governments had to agree to be terminated, and Lucy Covington was fighting to unseat the pro-termination council members, the "liquidators" as they were called, and get termination reversed.

So we went up to Colville and helped her put together an Indian paper called *Our Heritage*. It was an out-and-out propaganda sheet, and perhaps idealistically as an organization of journalists we should not have involved ourselves in a political campaign, but we thought it was a noble effort and we went ahead. That was what we called "advocacy journalism," and [we] thought it was valid in our world of siege mentality at that time. Objectivity was often a secondary consideration in those circumstances.

The federal government saw us as a potential tool for their policies. During the uprisings in the Yellow Thunder incident, for example, we were invited by the BIA to come to the Pine Ridge reservation to serve in the role of a rumor control function. That was the time, you may recall, when an Indian gentleman from Pine Ridge, Raymond Yellow Thunder, was humiliated and beaten to death by some young white thugs in Gordon, Nebraska, and the American Indian Movement came up to demonstrate against the racism that was rampant in those towns bordering the reservations. That was AIM's first move from urban areas into the reservations, and it scared the hell out of BIA to think that AIM was now invading what the BIA perceived as "their" territory.

Dick LaCourse and I went to Pine Ridge and, fortunately, we resisted the BIA's request to serve as a rumor control center and published some pretty good newspapers during that crisis. We got the story out about what was really behind the uprising, that it was not just AIM raising hell, but a growing number of grassroots people, including traditionals, who were fed up with being treated badly by whites, the federal government, and some of their own leaders.

It was interesting how we saw ourselves in those early years of AIPA. No doubt we saw ourselves as defenders of Indian people and Indian rights, as voices of Indian country. We saw ourselves fulfilling the people's right to know. There were differences among us, just like what might be facing ICA at times. There were differences in what our purposes should be, whether we should be about technical improvement or something more philosophical, or social, or political. But you should understand that those differences are to be expected from strong individuals, and that they are valid and reconcilable.

Looking back at those times, I see us as having been fearful of heresy and unwilling to question anything "Indian." I see ourselves as having been somewhat xenophobic in the fear of termination and abrogation of treaties. And we were appropriately angry, as the times seem to have called for, and that anger sometimes clouded our objectivity and reason. In that group we saw each other in the light of respect and kinship. We were very sensitive to one another in the Indian press, even to the point of avoiding anything that would cause unfair competition among newspapers. For example, there was discussion of perhaps pooling resources to publish a national Indian newspaper. That idea was rejected in favor of providing a news service to help improve the individual community newspapers across Indian country. Our concern was that a national paper would destroy local papers. We did consider a concept of a boilerplate national paper with regional inserts, which *Indian Country Today* now seems to be doing. The AIPA died somewhere back in the 1970's. I left the organization in 1972 to accept the position of executive director of the National Congress of American Indians, so I don't know the exact reasons for its demise. It may have had to do with its inability to raise funds among foundations, where the priorities were toward more activist and dramatic causes. The Indian press was seen by the foundations as pretty "establishment" during those heady times of revolution. I understand that there was also bickering among AIPA leaders, and there may have been problems of general mismanagement and non-payment of taxes. Even after its death, many Indian newspapers still carried the AIPA logo in their masthead. Later the Native American Journalists Association was created, which carries on what AIPA started years before. So I guess the lesson is that good ideas really don't die, but sometimes organizations do. ICA should guard against problems of bickering and mismanagement to ensure its continued existence.[25]

Bickering, as Trimble refers to it, may or may not be an appropriate way to describe the tensions that have arisen between ICA's Lower Forty-eight Natives and Alaska's Native broadcasters, or more specifically the Alaska Public Radio Network. ICA contends that APRN, which is a predominantly non-Indian organization, has thwarted its efforts to recruit Alaska's Indigenous broadcasters for the purpose of securing them a greater share of the state's public communications system funds.

Meanwhile, most Native Americans in Alaska remain supportive of APRN's practices and policies and are disinclined to buy ICA's argument that under the current non-Native system Indians are denied the level of participation they deserve. Although the debate had signs of developing into a turf war in 1994—a battle between North and South—ICA felt the clash of views would ultimately be reconciled to both party's satisfaction.

At the same time, fiscal and territorial issues have surfaced between ICA and NAPBC. One bone of contention has to do with the question of authority. For instance, ICA would like more autonomy when it comes to decisions regarding AIROS. However, Ray Cook and Frank Blythe see the relationship of the two organizations as essentially mutually beneficial.

Meanwhile, there is some dissatisfaction with the CPB Radio Production Fund. ICA would have prefered that the AIROS up-link facility and administration office be located at a reservation-based radio station, but CPB was disinclined to fund the operation on an Indian reserve where certain controls would likely have been relinquished, contends Ray Cook.

## PLANNED STATIONS

As of this writing, there are about a dozen and a half Native stations representing thirty-two Indigenous communities in the start-up or construction phase. This is the most since 1978, when CPB and NTIA inaugurated their Minority Station Start-up process and the FCC mandated the licensing of a greater number of minority-controlled broadcast outlets.

The count of Native radio frequencies will make a marked jump in the Midwest. For example, South Dakota will be the sight of a new high-powered Indian FM station in late 1995, if all goes according to plans, says KONA's development coordinator, Vince Two Eagles.

We have the frequency search completed and the land secured for the studio and tower. We're proposing a 100,000 watt FM station to be owned and operated by a private non-profit corporation called KONA Incorporated. Our primary audience will be the Native community, but we will not totally exclude the local non-Indian community by any means. We envision programming to include a mix of things: music, public affairs, news and information, weather, issues shows, and so on. KONA plans to be on the air from 6 A.M. to midnight and possibly longer in the future. KONA Incorporated would also like to look at the possibility of expanding to the AM band with the aim of a commercial broadcast venture as a means of developing a way to help defray the cost of running both facilities. The bottom line is that KONA wants to play a major role in preserving our culture, language, and way of life for future generations. The station will be a chartered non-profit organization through the state of South Dakota with specific permission from the Yankton Sioux Tribe to operate on the reservation by resolution.[26]

The Standing Rock Reservation, which spans both North and South Dakota borders, will be the site of another powerful Indian FM signal. The target date for 100,000-watt KAEN is late 1995. The station will be licensed to the seventh-generation Media Services Incorporated, which is "independent of the tribe yet closely connected to it,"[27] says Alex Looking Elk, who is the coordinator of the effort to put the station on the air.

KAEN plans a substantial amount of Native-language programming and culturally oriented programming. Like that of most Indigenous stations, its creation stems from a desire to fill the void on the radio dial where little exists to address the wants and needs of people residing on the remote reservation.

Meanwhile a station is being planned to serve the Sisseton Wahpeton Sioux tribe in South Dakota, and to the west and east of the state Native stations are in the works. In Wyoming the Arapahoo and Shoshone tribes on the Wind River Reservation are finally pursuing a broadcast license after failing to get the idea off the ground in the 1980s, when it was first proposed, and in Minnesota the Red Lake nations tribal council is engaged in a radio project.

In the southwest, KTNN plans to license another station to the Navajo nation. It would operate at 100,000 watts on the FM dial with the call letters KWRK. At this time, it has plans to broadcast rock and contemporary music to the Hopi and Navajo reservations. With this move its AM sister station plans to air a heavier schedule of Navajo-language programs.

Several Indigenous stations are being developed in Alaska, among them KBC in Anchorage. It will operate on the FM band and will be licensed to the Koahnic Broadcasting Corporation, a subsidiary of Cook Inlet Region Inc. The station intends to serve as a training ground for would-be Native broadcasters and a source for Indian programming for other state radio stations.

KBC plans to affiliate itself with the Alaska Public Radio Network and air locally produced news and public affairs features, as well as a broad mix of music.

Native stations are also planned for the Onondaga nation in New York State, Yakima Indian nation in Washington State, Gilla River Indians in Arizona, Santee Sioux tribe in South Dakota, and at the Cedar Unified School in Arizona, as well as at Fort Belknap College in Montana. The Lummi Corporation in Bellingham, Washington, is also working on a radio station project.

Several other communities are considering involvement with radio and have contacted ICA for assistance. They include the Acoma Pueblo of the Keresan tribe in New Mexico, Fort Peck tribes (Assiniboine and Sioux) in Montana, St. Regis Mohawk tribe in New York, Tohono O'odham nation in Arizona, All Indian Pueblo Council of New Mexico, Oneida tribe in Wisconsin, and the Red Lake band of Chippewa in Minnesota.

## CONCLUSION

Whatever the future is for broadcasting in America, it will include Indigenous people. While Native Americans may have come to the electronic media a half century behind everyone else—for reasons mostly beyond their control—their overdue presence will constitute a unique chapter (rather than a mere footnote) in future histories written about the Fifth Estate.

Indigenous broadcasters, as a team and as individuals, are making an important contribution to their own cultures, and they are enriching the appreciation of non-Indian America for those who live outside the mainstream. No longer will Indians be techno-peasants or media paupers but rather adept travelers on the information highway.

Charles Trimble eloquently describes the role of Native broadcasters in America, "Yours is a noble cause. You can free people. You can empower people. You can educate and inform people. You are an important part of the tribe."[28]

When it comes to recounting the Indian's past or forecasting what may lay ahead for The People, a simple but impassioned lyric from a Southwest tribal song perhaps says it best, "Tomorrow smiles, while sad was yesterday."

**ICA Joseph Orozco offers the following concluding thoughts on Indigenous broadcasting and its future.**

Recently I listened to National Public Radio's symposium discussion on the information highway. Where is this road going? Where is the on-ramp? What is the toll charge? Who are the gatekeepers? These are some of the questions that came to mind as I heard panel members addressing the issues.

While a member of the board of directors for the National Federation of Community Broadcasters, I took part in table discussions concerning the role of community radio. It seemed that as Vice President Al Gore drafted the outline for the great highway he and his techno-buddies did not think about public radio's involvement. When the staff of NFCB and others queried them on this, they said it was an oversight. I disagree. I think that the thought never occurred to them that radio broadcasting could in any way be of service to the land-line, fiber-optic driven info-highway.

My next question regarding the information highway is Will the information highway be open to Native broadcasters? If so, what role do we play? I have been talking this over with a few people over the years. At first our talks had nothing specifically to do with the information highway. We discussed possible activities a real Native media network could take on. These talks started during the early development of ICA. What can Native communities expect of a Native media network? What impact can be made by such an instrument? If Native communities hold the missing voice in national media, what message do we add to the mainstream? Do we use national media to run our versions of current national programs? Do we create a new paradigm in broadcast technique and content? Do we address all the above the best we can, and if so where do we start?

Thinking it over, I believe Native media must take the moral high ground. We create a new broadcasting paradigm. In doing so, we may run our own versions of non-Native programs, yet we still change the principles of self-expression. Program production will be talked about later. However, it should be noted here that a new broadcasting paradigm includes more than redesigning programs.

The current media standards place individuals in separate categories, such as producers, directors, writers, announcers, actors, and so forth. There are different associations or unions for each. There is a real pecking order at work here, and compensation levels vary greatly. Those at the top of the scale are indifferent to those below.

To create a healthy Native communication industry, we must change the paradigm so that each person is treated as an important part of the whole and compensated accordingly for his or her work.

### The Shaping of Things to Come

In late 1991 the talk about Native media centered on adding the missing voice to the mainstream discussion. We realized that radio was meant for Native people. We have a message to share. We have opinions about what is in the news. Our main problem was American mainstream society's inability to understand that there are other ways of thinking and viewing the world. This has always been the basic difference between Native and non-Native cultures. National news content was no different. How could it be any different? Who runs the national shows? Non-Natives. Who has easier access to national media systems? Non-Natives. Who chooses the news bites? Who chooses the news sources? Who chooses the news assignments? Again, non-Natives. This situation was about to change.

ICA was going to be our vehicle to address the world. Our first slogan was "Native Radio for the World." We envisioned a means to capitalize our network. Starting with CPB funding to organize a Native network by which CPB could communicate with Native communities, we immediately made plans to build upon the momentum. We saw how non-Natives have built media empires, and we figured we'd do the same. We could start out serving radio agendas, and as we grew we could systematically expand into other areas. If non-Natives have ABC, NBC, CBS, CNN, BET, NPR, APR, APRN, CPB, NFCB, and many others, why couldn't we compile our resources to create a national Native media network? This network could go beyond linking our Native communities together. It could go beyond sharing our insights on world events. This network could offer a new paradigm to national broadcasting.

## Recipe for Growth

Following this line of thought, ICA became a key way to create a future for Native Radio. If we linked the Native communities by radio and presented each radio entity as a strand of a web, we could net financial resources to address our development needs. This was the first ingredient in our recipe for growth.

By uniting all tribal stations under one umbrella, Native Radio in a plural sense was born. This arrangement allowed CPB, federal agencies, foundations, and corporations a way to fund larger project concepts that targeted greater numbers of Native people at one time. ICA then could regrant shares to all stations or subcontract project tasks to one or more stations. This is one way to create extra operating money for stations and build a service track record for ICA.

The creation of ICA as the cornerstone for a Native Radio network creates a beginning for a programming distribution center and related careers in the broadcast industry. The future of Native Radio began to reach over the horizon. We were seeing that it is possible to build a Native medium likened to the non-Native radio industry. We saw before us a means to make broadcast communications a viable career choice for our people.

## Along Comes AIROS

While we were searching for more funding resources and hoping for more financial breaks, CPB offered Native Radio money to research the viability of building a Native satellite system. CPB's thinking was, if it was to continue to fund Native programming, it only made sense that Native community stations should have a way to distribute these programs among themselves. ICA agreed.

However, we took the satellite concept a bit further. If we had the capability to share our CPB-funded programs among ourselves, we also would have the ability to share all our programs with the world. AIROS makes it possible to actualize our dreams. What we saw as topic areas for Native people to focus programming efforts on will constitute the missing voice on world affairs.

The future of Native Radio grows ever larger. We now see that beyond making available our program productions, we are looking to develop a myriad of broadcast support production careers. When we look at the support credits run on the television or movie screens, we envision similar jobs for Native people working in Native productions.

Just as the non-Native media industry started with radio and then developed into TV, cable, long-distance telephone relay systems, satellite communications, subcarrier systems, and fiber optics, we see a similar future for Native-based industry components.

## Technical Applications and Knowledge

The advantage Native Radio development has over non-Native radio experience is the fact that we were able to watch how people used the medium before we tried to create an industry of our own. As mentioned above, I think radio was made for Native people. By this I mean we have maintained an oral tradition. Indians can talk, and many of us have something to say.

As we build a future for Native Radio, we must look to what has happened in the world because of the media. The future holds a challenge for our integrity. Do we replicate what non-Native media have done? Or do we create a new paradigm?

These contrasting questions are only the tip of the iceberg. Before we go too much further, Native people must look into themselves. It is easy to see the technology at hand. It is easy to learn how to operate the equipment. It will be much harder to decide upon how we use our own media system.

In part, society blames the media for many ills. We too must be sensitive to the extent that we may add to the problem. If we wisely examine how media have been used, we could very well discover how to reverse some of the social disorders that exist. If such activity is our calling, we must not create a system that operates the same way the current non-Native system operates. If we want change, we must first change the way we operate.

The digital-technology systems can open many doors for us. Most of us in radio started out with analog equipment. Digital equipment will take us in two directions at once. First, digital equipment will allow us to produce faster and cleaner. That does not necessarily mean, however, that we'll be producing more material because second, the digital bandwidth will have many more paths to explore. The logical way to use digital technology's multiple paths efficiently is to train more people in the use of the overall system.

The future of Native Radio will be one of rapid expansion. It will be the equivalent of a black hole. It will take all the energy of today's Native Radio producers, engineers, programmers, editors, sound mixers, reporters, announcers, writers, schedulers, managers, development directors, program directors, publicists, linguists, coordinators, administrators, volunteers, and then some, to fill all the service applications digital technology makes available.

## We May Build Our Own On-Ramp

Native Radio in the future will expand beyond its current signals. What is heard today may still be heard. However, the digital frequencies allow much more available bandwidth per station. AIROS will play a huge role in the use of this space, and stations will play a big role in serving their communities with the added AIROS services.

Because of the inherent capabilities of digital technology, public broadcasting will eventually fragment into well-defined subcultures. Each subculture will be identified by the message it brings to the public. This means that radio in general will go the same way as the magazine industry. While radio may target specific populations now, in the future the messages it brings to the same target population will become more focused. Diversity broadcasting as we know it today will pale by comparison to that which will be transmitted on the digital spectrum. Because of the new capabilities of digital service, public radio will open another multichannel lane on the superhighway. This possibility is what Gore's panel failed to foresee. One of the major problems of the land-line information highway is the fact that the American public already travels from point to point by car, train, metro, bus, van, or boat or on foot. It is very difficult to remain plugged into a landline system while one is on the go. That's where digital radio satellite systems come into play. They are the on-ramp.

## The Highway Is a Tollway

Native Radio then evolves into Native telecommunications. All of the jobs currently held at radio stations will be absorbed and redefined to meet digital standards and aspirations. More jobs in telecommunication will be created by the imaginations of those who want to be involved. What we understand as radio programs today will spin off into multimedia programs tomorrow, just as old-time radio theater spun off into TV sitcoms.

The American public will always want to know what is happening in the world. Looking at today's media choices, people seem discontent with the content of national news service offerings. We are seeing more and more specialized interview shows and magazine-type broadcast productions. This trend will likely continue and expand.

The American public will continue to move about the country. Even though communication networks bring people together for meetings via satellite and fiber optics, they will not be able to recreate that face-to-face, look-me-in-the-eye contact that is a major part of nonverbal communications. This contact will require people to travel. People will still need to tap into media channels while on the run. Public tele-radio will bring them what they want, when they want it.

Just as we currently have Muzak, Reading for the Blind, language-learning channel, chain store inventory systems, and the like, we will be able to connect the everyday citizen to his or her nearest public tele-radio base for the latest news and analysis information. We will be able to connect the user to unlimited sources with a handheld multimedia receiver.

## Adding Medicinal Herbs to the Stew

The future of Native Radio is all of the above. Are we ready for this journey? The AIROS project has brought to our attention the thinness of our production capabilities. Using the current standards of actual broadcast time as a measurement tool, Native Radio cannot fill twelve hours of broadcast time per day. It may take a year or more to build up our inventories enough to fill this void. The production problem is not the real issue, however. What really gets in the way of fulfilling our dream is the lack of acknowledgment by tribal governments. They fail to see Native Radio's value.

Tribes have poured millions of dollars into industries based on natural resources that have reduced the cultural wealth of our lands. This was done because these activities created hugh profits and well-paying jobs for unemployed tribal members. While the big bucks went to the harvesting of natural resources, small allowances went to the tribe's radio stations. The undervaluation of radio by tribal governments tells its people that broadcasting is a dead-end job. Until tribal governments invest equal amounts of money in communication, as they have done in forestry, mining, housing, and so on, parents will not encourage their children to pursue the kinds of courses they will need to be successful communicators.

The need not to replicate the standards and practices of non-Native media systems has been mentioned. Native broadcasters must also take care to avoid replicating the governance systems used in tribal affairs when they design the governance structures of a national Native media system.

The development of Native Radio depends on the health of all the individual Native stations. The AIROS system may one day absorb ICA, or it may be the other way around. However, in either case, it will be the strength of the Native stations that shapes their future.

# Afterword: A Native Producer's Perspective

by Peggy Berryhill

Indian voices on the radio permeate my summer memories. When I was a little girl visiting my sister in Montana, I can remember hearing voices speaking Crow and Cheyenne on stations in Forsyth and Miles City. It was on trips through Arizona and New Mexico during our annual pilgrimage from California back to the Creek nation in Oklahoma that I first heard Navajo and Apache on the air. These languages sounded so different from the Muskogee spoken at home by my parents. These Indian voices were always on *commercial* radio stations, sometimes on a Sunday morning slot shared with community news (usually interspersed with English-speaking commercials), gospel, and country and western music.

Today we see the growth of *public* radio stations on Indian reservations. Right now we have twenty-five public radio stations on the air and several more will go on the air in the next few years. That's what *Signals in the Air* is about—the public radio phenomenon. Telecommunications has been called the "new Indian movement." All over America, Indian people are speaking to their own communities in their own languages. New forums, beamed by satellite, are opening up the rural borders of reservations, stretching the boundaries that have kept Indian communities from sharing their cultures, philosophies, and current events with the rest of America and the world. Whether it is by running their own radio stations, producing television programs, or telecommuting on the great information highway, Native people are doing for themselves what cannot be accomplished by the mainstream media. They are sharing their communities' concerns in their own voices, uninterrupted by cultural interpreters and reporters who lack the background to understand the complex issues of contemporary Native life, issues such as gaming, sovereignty, jurisdiction, and religious freedom.

In the 1970s I began what was to become my vocation—broadcasting. I didn't know that I would come to be known as the "First Lady" of Indian radio or the unofficial "queen" of Indian radio, as some have called me. I had no idea at that time that I would spend the next two decades of my life visiting dozens of Indian communities, racking up hundreds of thousands of air and land miles, recording thousands of hours of audio tape, and leaving a trail of acquaintances behind in my passion to bring the voices of Indian people to public radio.

While my equipment has changed (from analog to digital), the drive to produce programming from a Native perspective and to break down stereotypes by sharing the voices and visions from many Indian communities has never waned. One of the hidden stories in public broadcasting history is the battle to bring community perspectives to the airwaves, unedited, untranslated, untouched by well-meaning folks who are driven by the mainstream marketplace to reduce culture to soundbites. For decades Native peoples' only access to the airwaves has been to produce news and documentaries. Indeed, most of the work that I have done has been in these particular formats.

I remember back in the 1970s having a heated argument with the managing editor at National Public Radio about the need for more mainstream coverage of Indian issues by Indian reporters. The news director (long since gone from NPR) told me that it would never be acceptable to have blacks report on black issues or women on women's issues and certainly not Indians on Indian issues, because they couldn't be objective reporters. (There was not much chance of that happening back in those days anyway since the majority of reporters were white men with a few white women at the forefront.) I asked him why then did they have only white men covering Congress, which at that time was almost exclusively white and male. He turned heel and stormed away from me—end of argument.

It was while working as a producer at National Public Radio that I began my intimate involvement with Native radio. In 1978 there were about eight or nine Native-controlled stations on air, and they played NPR's documentary series *Horizons*. I was a producer for *Horizons* and worked on programs submitted by independent producers as well as my own programs. It was because of this documentary work that I began to get calls from the Native stations. Bernie Bustos of KTDB (then located in the Navajo community of Ramah) would call and ask "What [program] have you got for me this week?" Other managers would invite me to come out and train their producers. Having come from a community radio background myself and understanding the pitfalls of relying on listener support and grants to maintain a funding base, I grew concerned for Native radio. It was in the 1970s that I dedicated myself to help out in whatever way I could. Envisioning an army of Native radio producers, I began going to the stations and have been blessed to have visited a few repeatedly.

One of the first stops along the path was to visit KSHI in Zuni, New Mexico. I worked with Susan Braine (then the general manager) and her staff, which included Faye Eriacho and Duane Chimoni (KSHI's current manager). I'll never forget the first thing Faye said to me after meeting me and being surprised that I was an Indian: "Well, we always wondered who that white woman was that produced such good programs for Indians." We all had a good laugh over that one! Over the years I have been to Zuni many times and most recently worked again with Faye on the taping of the Department of Justice's Indian Listening Conference of May 1994.

Way back in the 1970s, Susan Braine and I became the first to call attention to the needs of Indian radio, and we have become friends for life. Susan is now the manager of the American Indian Radio on Satellite network located in Lincoln, Nebraska. AIROS is a joint project of the Native American Public Broadcasting Consortium and the Indigenous Communications Association. One of its goals is to provide Native programming in a variety of formats to all of public radio.

My training paths have taken me to most of the Native stations, and I've seen a tremendous amount of turnover of staff, although a few people have managed to stay on board. I've seen WOJB's Camille Lacapa-Morrison grow into the role of general manager after starting out in the receptionist area as a secretary. I treasure a WOJB T-shirt designed by Camille, who is a gifted artist. At KMHA in North Dakota, I have seen Pete Coffey, Jr., and Nina Fox grow and continue to produce cultural programs for their communities, earning the respect of their people along the way. Nina is now the manager at KMHA and Pete is the program director. KTDB's Bernie Bustos, Barbara Maria, and Irene Beaver and KABR's Patsy Apachito are often in my thoughts as I work on project after project. It is my involvement with all stations along the way that has kept me strong and renewed my spirit to produce as I have battled for airtime for Native programs.

For the most part, programs labeled minority have been ghettoized for decades by the primary distributors of public radio programming. For many years I have produced documentaries that have been distributed under the umbrella of "minority and/or specialized audience" program streams. For decades I have been told by public radio station managers, all very nice people, that Indian programs were "not for their audience," but they "sympathized with our cause." And for decades I have continued to insist on marketing programs to mainstream stations and have ignored the voices of the naysayers. As a result, many of my programs have been honored with awards. The *Spirits* series has been sold through catalogs and national bookstores, and the *Red Road* (produced by the Hazelden Foundation) has been a big seller and, more important, has helped many people to heal—both Indian and non-Indian. These successes show that the audience for Native American programs is widespread.

As an Indian, I knew that there was a tremendous interest in our people, our cultures, our histories, and our lifeways. As a producer, I have continually fought for quality time slots, not Sunday morning 6 A.M. or Wednesday night 10 P.M. slots reserved for "minority" programs. One of the biggest battles we wage as Native producers is against stereotypes. This struggle is on-going.

There have been many positive changes in Indian images, but the old ideas persist in portraying Indian people as tragic victims speaking only broken English, as pitiful alcoholics, as angry militants, and as mythical spiritual beings. You will still primarily hear stories about the Sioux or Lakota people and the Navajo accompanied by drum music and lyrical flutes. The other 700 plus tribes and communities are rarely depicted anywhere. The fact that we have many well-educated tribal leaders governing their communities goes unreported. Sometimes I feel like an Indian "411" service as I am called by teachers wanting information and CNN for tips on whom to ask about certain issues. I have never seen or heard the results of these inquiries. It was because of the persistence of these stereotypes that in 1990 we began production of a major project that would be the voice of Indian communities.

It was called *Spirits of the Present: the Legacy from Native America.* It was distributed in 1992, and I was the coordinating producer. This was a joint production of the Native American Public Broadcasting Consortium and the Smithsonian Institution's Office of Telecommunications. We also sought the input of hundreds of Indian people. We produced a thirteen-week series that was carried by an unprecedented 427 stations across the United States and Canada! We shared the voices of 150 Native people: teachers, lawyers, spiritual leaders, elders, and youth from more than 50 urban and rural communities. The enthusiasm of our team at the Smithsonian and the support of the NAPBC and our distributor, American Public Radio, brought Indian programming to the forefront for one season in 1992 during the

United States quincentennial year. The best reward for three years of hard work has been hearing from Indian people who have told me of their pride and joy at hearing the programs.

In the same way *Spirits* was tied to the 1992 quincentennial, most Indian programs have been marketed by linking them to holidays, like Thanksgiving or Columbus Day. (This is also true for other cultural programs, for example during February, which is Black History Month, you will find a plethora of African American cultural offerings.) Most documentaries by their nature tend to be issue oriented—examinations of topics layered with "talking heads." There has been very little room for political and philosophical forums that feature the Native American intelligentsia. There has been virtually no room for mainstream distribution of the eloquent speechmaking by Native elders and political leaders and only a smattering of airtime has been given to the voices of our poets, writers, artists, and musicians.

In the same way that a film is reduced to a synopsis of plot and character description on mainstream news shows, so have Native issues been reduced to soundbites and minimal content with regard to providing the non-Indian listener with a true understanding of the politics of Indian sovereignty or religious freedom. Culture is more than a soundbite and today's marketplace has placed too much emphasis on news immediacy.

Where is there room for the cross-cultural dialogue that we all need today in America? On the AM dial we are surrounded by talk show hosts who play to the lowest common denominators, yet these people are seen as influential cultural barometers. On mainstream public radio we get the highly educated, informed analyst, but this individual is someone who is often lacking in real world experience. Who will make room on their stations for the other voices, the other formats in these days when competition for the dollar squeezes out any program that might turn off listeners?

In this book, Michael Keith delved into the funding pit. It is there that all program producers, large production organizations with multimillion-dollar budgets as well as the single independent producer, must compete for a share of the pot. Over the years the most victorious formats to emerge with funding are the news and documentary formats. The animal that has become mainstream media has turned news programming into the king of the hill. I will not argue against the need for quality news programs, but I will continue to argue for a place on the airwaves for programs that reflect all cultural traditions in American society.

Until we place the product of our Native American audio artists on the same level as our graphic artists, basket makers, dancers, and potters, we will continue to miss the opportunity to fully appreciate the value of this new art form and embrace all things Indian. The time has come when radio will encompass all Native nations and no boundaries will separate the voices of our youth, elders, aunts, and uncles, whether urban or rural, from the northern or southern hemispheres. Native radio cannot stand alone. It is part of a whole system that encompasses all aspects of culture and feeds the technology that carries the messages. When you consider that we have more than 700 Indian communities, many that will never have a radio or television station, you can see the need for the AIROS network to enable both stations and producers to carry the Indian message to all people.

As the century closes and we find urban and rural communities grappling with broadcast technologies that promise "interaction" and "on-line communities," we still find radio at the forefront of human interaction. Native stations will take their place along side all the other media linked by the common bonds of community, and they will do for Native people what the mainstream cannot. We will still be Indians or Native Americans or "the People," but we will not be reduced to a soundbite or a 6 A.M. Sunday morning time slot.

*Appendix*

# Telecommunications Technology and Native Americans: Opportunities and Challenges

In April 1994, Senator Daniel K. Inouye, Chairman, Senate Committee on Indian Affairs, requested that the Office of Technology Assessment (OTA) prepare a report for Congress which evaluated telecommunications applications and uses in Indian Country within the context of the impending National Information Infrastructure.

What follows is the text of the proposal, whose completed report was due April 1995. Information from this book was used in the preparation of the Inouye study.

## IMPORTANCE OF THE PROPOSAL

Native Americans—including American Indians, Alaska Natives, and Native Hawaiians—face continuing challenges in achieving social and economic independence. Native communities typically are geographically remote and must cope with high levels of unemployment and social distress. Native Americans have a heritage of self-sufficiency, and are seeking to regain control over their lives and futures. The thrust of U.S. Government policy today is to assist Native Americans in their quest for self-determination, and to help them develop the community infrastructure that will support healthy families and viable local economies. Many Native American communities—such as American Indian reservations and Alaska Native villages—are assuming responsibility for services and functions (e.g., education, health, public safety, and economic development) previously carried out by government agencies.

In recent years, some Native American leaders have recognized the potential of telecommunications and computing technologies to help revitalize their communities. Farsighted leaders and grassroots activists have sponsored or conducted pilot tests, seminars, and small-scale projects that demonstrate how Native Americans can use these technologies to help improve their social and economic conditions. But at the same time, the pace of technological and policy changes has increased markedly and threatens to outstrip the fragile beginnings of Native American self-sufficiency in information technology.

The United States—in both government and private sectors—is accelerating development of a national information infrastructure (NII). Some early elements of the NII, such as computer networking, are already rapidly expanding. Federal, state, and local governments are aggressively developing, testing, and, increasingly, implementing electronic delivery of services.

There is great risk, however, that Native Americans—among other disadvantaged or distressed segments of U.S. society—will be bypassed by the NII and fail to capture the benefits of telecommunications and computing for their social ad economic livelihood. This proposed study would focus on the factors and policy options that could help assure the effective participation of Native Americans in the ongoing information technology revolution and bring the technology to bear in ways that would improve their communities, families, and economic prospects.

## CONGRESSIONAL AND RELATED INTEREST

This proposed study is of direct interest to the Senate Committee on Indian Affairs, the requester. The Committee is exploring the potential of telecommunications technology to, for example, facilitate economic and social development in Native American communities. The study will likely be of interest to the House Committee on Natural Resources and its Subcommittee on Native American Affairs, that likewise desires to enhance the economic and social conditions of Native Americans. Aspects of the study focusing on access of Native Americans to telecommunications services and networks also will likely be of interest to committees with jurisdiction over telecommunications policies (e.g., Senate Committee on Commerce, Science, and Transportation, House Committee on Energy and Commerce). Parts of the study examining opportunities for electronic delivery of Federal services to Native Americans also will likely be of interest to committees with jurisdiction over relevant services (e.g., for educational services, the Senate Committee on Labor and Human Resources and House Committee on Education and Labor). The study also will be of interest to those concerned about the economic and social conditions of Native Americans, and the use of information technology in meeting Native American needs, including: a) organizations representing the Nation's Native Americans; b) individual Native American communities, villages, and reservations; and c) government, consumer, self-help, business, economic development, and other groups and organizations involved with Native Americans.

## SISTER AGENCY COORDINATION

GAO, CBO, and CRS are not conducting or planning studies on this topic. GAO and CRS are conducting studies on related issues such as American Indian housing, health care, and employment conditions. These study results will be used as background information to the extent appropriate.

## TOPICS TO BE ADDRESSED

The study will focus on opportunities for Native Americans—including American Indians, Alaska Natives, and Native Hawaiians—to use information technology to improve their social and economic conditions, and the policies and initiatives that could help them take advantage of opportunities identified.

The study will address:

1. *Native American traditions, culture, community, and governance relevant to use of information technology.* From the outset, it is important to understand the factors that encourage or inhibit the use of information technology by Native Americans in their communities. Some factors may be generic to many technology users; others may be unique to Native Americans. The study will examine the roles of organizations and activists in using or promoting information technology at the grassroots level, including: schools and colleges; libraries; community centers; social service agencies; entrepreneurs; and telephone, cable, and computer companies.

2. *Opportunities for application of telecommunication and computing technologies to meet Native American needs.* Not all needs are relevant to, or can be addressed through, the application of technology. The key is to identify areas of need in which the use of information technology can be leveraged (along with other factors such as training and facilitators) to make

a significant difference—at least in concept. This activity will include a review of prior research and pilot projects to determine the factors that will contribute to successful use of these technologies by Native Americans. The study will consider the range of technologies and issues outlined in OTA's 1993 report *Making Government Work*, as they apply to Native American communities.

3. *Prospects for information technology-based economic development and job creation in Native American communities.* High unemployment is a source and symptom of much distress among Native Americans. Lack of jobs contributes to near-poverty conditions and social problems for many. Inadequate education, health services, and community infrastructure impedes economic development. What is the combination of factors needed—including appropriate use of information technology—to turn this situation around? What are the optimistic expectations for and realistic limitations on the role of information technology? The study will review current public and private sector technology-based activities directed toward improving the socioeconomic conditions of Native Americans.

4. *Telecommunications and information policy issues and options relevant to Native Americans.* Native Americans have a lot in common with people in rural and inner city areas when it comes to telecommunications and information policy. Policy development is historically driven by technology applications and industry initiatives to meet the needs of the more affluent sectors of American society—those with the greatest ability to pay for and use new technologies. The Federal Government, among others, has asserted itself through a variety of policies, regulations, and programs to help reduce the gap between economically or educationally advantaged citizens and those less so. These Federal policies and programs are under pressure from the rapid pace of technology and market advances, tightening fiscal constraints, and the growing movement to "reinvent" government.

The study will address the following questions: What policy issues are most critically linked to preserving or improving the equity of access of Native Americans to telecommunication and computer technologies and to strengthening the ability of Native Americans to use these technologies for their own betterment? What current and prospective public policy initiatives on the national information infrastructure, telecommunications deregulation, and electronic service delivery could affect Native Americans and how? In what ways can telecommunications and information policies work most synergistically with programs for Native American community, educational, and economic development? How can information technology be used to improve the delivery of Federal services (e.g., health) to Native

Americans, and to perhaps reinvent the roles of the responsible agencies (e.g., Indian Health Service, Bureau of Indian Affairs)? What policy options offer greatest leverage in helping the U.S. Government carry out its treaty and statutory obligations to Native Americans? What individual options, or combinations of options, warrant congressional consideration? To what extent can the policy conclusions from this study be generalized to other segments of American society?

# Notes

## CHAPTER 1

1. E. B. Eiselein, *Indian Issues* (Blackfoot Nation, Mont.: Spirit Talk Press, 1993), p. 132.

2. The Dawes Act, passed by Congress in 1887, sought to "civilize" Indians by eliminating communal land ownership and allotting individual Indians prescribed amounts of acreage for cultivation.

3. Eiselein, p. 3.

4. Marlita A. Reddy, ed. *Statistical Record of Native North Americans* (Detroit: Gale Research, 1993).

5. Bruce Smith and Jerry Brigham, "Native Radio Broadcasting in North America: An Overview of Systems in the United States and Canada," *Journal of Broadcasting and Electronic Media*, spring 1992, p. 184.

6. Eiselein, p. 4.

7. Reddy, p. 274.

8. Ray Cook, letter to author, 22 January 1994.

9. Frank Blythe, telephone interview by author, 8 January 1994.

10. Theodore Grame, *Ethnic Broadcasting in the United States* (Washington, D.C.: American Folklife Center), p. 83.

11. Karen Holp, telephone interview by author, 10 January 1994.

12. Ibid.

13. Bob Harmon, letter to author, 20 October 1993.

14. Ibid.

15. Deborah Wright, letter to author, 7 January 1994.

16. Cook.

17. Deborah Alstrom, letter to author, 6 October 1993.

18. Nellie Vale, letter to author, 17 November 1993.

19. Jim Pidrock, letter to author, 27 November 1993.

20. *Broadcasting and Cable Yearbook*, 1992, pp. A-314 to A-317.

21. *Broadcasting and Cable*, 14 March 1994, p. 66.

22. Ibid.

23. James E. Murphy. "Alaska Native Communications Media: An Overview," *Gazette*, 1982, p. 97.

24. Smith and Brigham, p. 183.

25. Cook.

26. This 30-minute program is provided by Oklahomans for Indian Opportunities (OIO), a group devoted to finding solutions to the problems Native Americans face in contemporary society. It is hosted and produced by Michael Dodson, who interviews guests on topics ranging from art and heritage to health and governance.

27. Mary Murdock, letter to author, 4 January 1994.

28. Michael Askins, letter to author, 14 December 1993.

29. Martha Demaree, letter to author, 18 December 1993.

30. Scott Kooistra, letter to author, 8 December 1993.

31. George Reichman, letter to author, 19 December 1993.

32. The 1992 *Broadcasting and Cable Yearbook* lists only three Anglo stations that devote their programming schedules to Native Americans.

33. Dale Felkner in *Radio Programming: Consultancy and Formatics* by Michael C. Keith (Stoneham, Mass.: Focal Press, 1987), p. 171.

34. Jim Maiorano, letter to author, 9 October 1993.

35. Grame, p. 82.

36. Ibid., p. 83.

37. Ibid., p. 83.

38. Peggy Berryhill, telephone interview by author, 30 December 1993.

39. Telephone interview by author, 29 December 1993.

40. Cook.

41. Argie O'Shea of NPR Promotion and Marketing, telephone interview by author, 28 December 1993.

42. Gary Fife in "Smithsonian Collects Broadcasts," by Sheila Toomey, *Anchorage Daily News*, 21 October 1993, p. E-3.

43. Julia Rubin. "Reporter Covers American Indians for Public Radio," *Argus Leader*, 2 June 1991, p. 6AA.

44. *ICA Newsletter*, July 1992.

45. Leigh-Ann M. Gerow, letter to author, 8 December 1993.

46. E B. Eiselein, letter to author, January 1994.

47. Ruby Calvert, program director, KCWC, telephone interview by author, 7 January 1994.

## CHAPTER 2

1. Eiselein, *Indian Issues*, p. 10.

2. Ibid.

3. Ibid., p. 11.

4. Ibid., p. 12.

5. Ibid., p. 13.

6. Wilma Mankiller and Michael Wallis, *Mankiller: A Chief and Her People* (New York: St. Martin's Press, 1993), p. 161.

7. Vine Deloria, Jr., *Behind the Trail of Broken Treaties* (New York: Delacourt, 1974).

8. Peter Matthiessen, *In the Spirit of Crazy Horse* (New York: Viking, 1983, 1991), p. 35.

9. Dale Means, telephone interview by author, 18 December 1993.

10. Matthiessen, p. 36.

11. Vine Deloria, Jr., *Custer Died for Your Sins: An Indian Manifesto* (Norman: University of Oklahoma Press, 1969), p. x.

12. Simon Ortiz, "Speaking of Courage," *A Circle of Nations* (Hillsboro, Ore.: Beyond Words Publishing, 1993), p. 27.

13. Francis Paul Prucha, *The Indians in American Society* (Berkeley: University of California Press, 1985), p. 83.

14. Herman Viola, *After Columbus* (Washington, D.C.: Smithsonian Books, 1990), p. 247.

15. Vernon Bellecourt, telephone interview by author, 12 December 1993.

16. Ray Cook, telephone interview by author, 3 January 1994.

17. Mark Tilsen, telephone interview by author, 18 December 1993.

18. Gerald Vizenor in *Native American Testimony* by Peter Nabokov (New York: Penguin Books, 1978, 1991), p. 380.

19. Francis Paul Prucha, letter to author, 24 December 1993.

20. Mankiller and Wallis, p. 188.

21. Eiselein, *Indian Issues*, p. 13.

22. Ray Cook, letter to author, 10 January 1994.

23. Mary Dinota, public broadcasting consultant, letter to author, 9 December 1993.

24. Holp.

25. Mark Trahant, "Friends, We Are All Indians," *A Circle of Nations*, p. 60.

26. Smith and Brigham, p. 184.

27. Eiselein, *Indian Issues*, p. 65.

28. Ibid., p. 128.

29. J. Fred MacDonald, *Don't Touch That Dial: Radio Programming in American Life from 1920 to 1960* (Chicago: Nelson-Hall, 1979), p. 205.

30. Deloria, *Custer Died for Your Sins*, p. 201.

31. Erik Barnouw, *The Image Empire: A History of Broadcasting in the United States from 1953*, vol. 3 (New York: Oxford University Press, 1970), pp. 170–71.

32. Rose W. Robinson, letter to author, 8 December 1993.

33. Allen Myers, telephone interview by author, 1 January 1994.

34. Smith and Brigham, p. 184.

35. Robinson.

36. Ray Cook, "Mohawk Nation Radio," *NFCB Community Radio News*, August 1991, pp. 3–4.

37. Wayne Bundy, New Mexico broadcast pioneer, telephone interview by author, 6 December 1993.

38. Wilbur Paul, Cherokee Agency BIA superintendent, letter to author, 6 October 1993.

39. John A. McDonald, KYUK general manager, letter to author, 21 September 1993.

40. Carol Standing Elk, telephone interview by author, 14 December 1993.

41. Cook, "Mohawk Nation Radio," p. 3.

42. Ibid.

43. Eiselein, *Indian Issues*, p. 28.

44. Ibid., p. 138.

45. Allen Myers, letter to author, 10 January 1994.

46. Ray Cook, interview by author, 22 December 1993.

47. Joseph Orozco, telephone interview by author, 17 February 1994.

## CHAPTER 3

1. Dinota.

2. Lynn Chadwick, letter to author, 27 December 1993.

3. Peter M. Lewis and Jerry Booth, *The Invisible Medium* (Washington, D.C.: Howard University Press, 1990), p. 121.

4. ICA membership brochure.

5. Ray Cook, letter to author, 13 January 1994.

6. Ray Cook, Final Interim Report on ICA Activity, 13 January 1994.

7. Ray Cook, telephone interview by author, 11 January 1994.

8. ICA manifesto, recorded by Joseph Orozco.

9. IBC media kit statement.

10. Ibid.

11. NAPBC brochure.

12. Dwight M. Ellis, letter to author, 13 January 1994.

13. Lynn Christian, telephone interview by author, 14 November 1993.

14. Bruce Smith and Jerry Brigham, unpublished manuscript.

15. Bruce Smith and Jerry Brigham, letter to author, 22 January 1994.

16. Orozco.

17. Ibid.

18. Smith and Brigham, unpublished manuscript.

19. Nan Rubin, "Final Report on the Native American Training Project," 1987, pp. 5–7.

20. Orozco.

21. Cook, telephone interview by author, 9 January 1994.
22. Eiselein, *Indian Affairs*, p. 130.
23. Cook, letter.
24. Delfred Smith, letter to author, 24 January 1994.
25. Smith and Brigham, "Native Radio Broadcasting," Table 1.
26. Charles Trimble, from keynote speech to ICA at NFCB conference, 1994.
27. Eiselein, *Indian Affairs*, p. 130.
28. WYRU station profile sheet.
29. Al Stone, telephone interview by author, 30 December 1993.
30. Ibid.
31. Dale Gehman, telephone interview by author, 29 December 1993.
32. Ibid.
33. Ibid.
34. Ibid.
35. Ibid.
36. Broadcasting Unlimited market report, 1986, p. 32.
37. Ibid., p. 33.
38. Ibid., pp. 33–34.
39. Ibid., p. 34.
40. Ibid., p. 35.
41. Delfred Smith.
42. John Stolz, letter to author, 15 December 1994.
43. Stu Schader, letter to author, 22 January 1994.
44. Barbara Maria, letter to author, 2 December 1993.
45. Duane Chimoni, letter to author, 30 November 1993.
46. Joseph Gill, letter to author, 17 January 1994.
47. Bruce Smith, letter to author, 8 January 1994.
48. Susan Braine, letter to author, 14 November 1993.
49. Bob Sommer, letter to author, 6 January 1994.
50. Eiselein, letter.
51. "Broadcast and Cable Employment Report," 7 June 1993, p. 2.
52. Braine.

# CHAPTER 4

1. Smith and Brigham, "Native Radio Broadcasting," Table 1.
2. E. B. Eiselein. "Who Is Listening to Native Public Radio?" (Kalispell, Mont.: A & A Research, 1992), p. 1. Report prepared for CPB.
3. Cook, Final Interim Report, p. 5.
4. Eiselein, "Who Is Listening?" p. 3.
5. Ibid., p. 2.
6. McDonald.

7. This material appeared in *NFCB Community Radio News*, July 1993. Lightly edited.

8. KTDB station brochure.

9. Barbara Maria, letter to author, 12 October 1993.

10. Bob Rawls, letter to author, 1 November 1993.

11. Len Anderson, telephone interview by author, 1 March 1994.

12. Ibid.

13. Betty Hamley, letter to author, 27 October 1993.

14. Ibid.

15. Dorene R. Bruce, letter to author, 29 October 1993.

16. This material appeared in *NFCB Community Radio News*, June 1990. Lightly edited.

17. "The KBRW Bulletin," fall 1992.

18. Don Rinker, letter to author, 24 September 1993.

19. This material appeared in *NFCB Community Radio News*, January 1991. Lightly edited.

20. Chimoni.

21. This material appeared in *NFCB Community Radio News*, November 1991. Lightly edited.

22. Smith and Brigham, "Native Radio Broadcasting," Table 1.

23. Eiselein, *Indian Issues*, p. 1.

24. This material appeared in *NFCB Community Radio News*, January 1993. Lightly edited.

25. Camille Lacapa-Morrison, letter to author, 20 September 93.

26. This material appeared in *NFCB Community Radio News*, January 1990. Lightly edited.

27. Phoebe Nez, letter to author, 6 October 1993.

28. *Boston Globe Magazine*, 26 November 1989, p. 30.

29. Tom Casey, telephone interview by author, 13 October 1993.

30. Mike Her Many Horses, telephone interview by author, 14 November 1993.

31. Delbert Brewer, letter to author, 16 November 1993.

32. Means.

33. This material appeared in *NFCB Community Radio News*, February 1993. Lightly edited.

34. Pete Coffey, Jr., letter to author, 22 October 1993.

35. Terrance Walters, letter to author, 26 October 1993.

36. This material appeared in *NFCB Community Radio News*, July 1992. Lightly edited.

37. Eiselein, *Indian Affairs*, p. 1.

38. *NFCB Community Radio News*, August 1991.

39. Smith and Brigham, unpublished manuscript, p. 13.

40. Warren Cassador, telephone interview by author, 7 March 1994.

41. Bill Ziegler, telephone interview by author, 4 December 1993.

42. Janet Sauer, letter to author, 17 January 1994.

43. Ibid.

44. Ibid.

45. Delfred Smith.

46. Doug Letch, telephone interview by author, 6 March 1994.

47. Ibid.

48, Susan Braine, letter to author, 11 November 1993.

## CHAPTER 5

1. Dee Brown, *Bury My Heart at Wounded Knee* (New York: Henry Holt & Company, 1970), p. 316.

2. Joseph Gill, letter to author, 12 January 1994.

3. Jerry Kramer, *Arizona Republic*, 7 June 1993, p. A2.

4. Nan Rubin, pp. 13–14.

5. Peterson Zah, letter to author, 4 November 1993.

6. Anna Kosof, "Public Radio—Americans Want More." *Media Studies Journal*, summer 1993, p. 173.

7. Robinson.

8. Bruce Smith, letter to author, 6 January 1994.

9. Leonard Burch, telephone interview by author, 30 November 1993.

10. Alex Lunderman, letter to KINI general manager, 21 January 1988.

11. Marvin Molson, letter to author, 8 October 1993.

12. Delbert Brewer, letter to author, 27 October 1993.

13. Bruce.

14. Walters.

15. Barbara Maria, letter to author, 6 November 1993.

16. Bob Sommer, letter to author, 8 November 1993.

17. From a KIYU survey in the early 1990s.

18. From a KIYU survey.

19. Robin L. Claymore, letter to author, 25 October 1993.

20. Eiselein, letter.

21. Nan Rubin, pp. 12–13.

22. Ibid., p. 11.

23. Evelyn James, letter to author, 29 October 1993.

24. Eiselein, letter.

25. Nan Robin, p. 11.

26. Ibid., p. 20.

27. Corey Flintoff, letter to author, 20 September 1993.

28. John McDonald, letter to author, 21 September 1993.

29. Eiselein, letter.

30. Bellecourt.

31. Luci Tapahonso, "The Kan River Rushes Westward," *A Circle of Nations* (Hillsboro, Ore.: Beyond Words Publishing, 1993), p. 108.

32. Curley Biggs, telephone interview by author, 30 November 1993.

33. Alfred Trepania, telephone interview by author, 30 November 1993.

34. Patsy Apachita, letter to author, 4 September 1993.

35. Maria, letter, 6 November 1993.

36. Eiselein, letter.

37. Peter Nabokov, *Native American Testimony* (New York: Penguin Books, 1992), p. 418.

38. Mike Her Many Horses, telephone interview by author, 30 November 1993.

39. Burch.

40. President to the Ramah Navajo tribe, telephone interview by author, 30 November 1993.

41. Mike Her Many Horses.

42. Michael Jandreau, telephone interview by author, 30 November 1993.

43. Robinson.

44. Standing Elk.

45. KTDB station survey, 10 July 1991.

46. Eiselein, "Who Is Listening?" pp. 7–15.

47. Camille Lacapa-Morrison, letter to author, 20 September 1993.

48. Mike Her Many Horses, telephone interview.

49. Eiselein, *Indian Issues*, p. 131.

50. Joseph Orozco, letter to author, 20 February 1994.

51. Bellecourt.

52. Michael Goldberg, letter to author, 7 December 1993.

53. Nan Rubin, pp. 13–14.

54. Eiselein, *Indian Issues*, p. 138.

55. Eiselein, letter.

56. From station KTNN's media kit.

57. Sent to KINI by a mainstream station owner and manager.

58. Sent to KINI by CBS News correspondent.

59. Sent to KINI by the South Dakota Department of Health.

## CHAPTER 6

1. Kallen M. Martin, letter to author, 7 November 1993.

2. Coffey.

3. Susan Braine, letter to author, 10 November 1993.

4. ICA brochure and Ray Cook, letter to author, 17 May 1994.

5. Eiselein, letter.

6. Ray Cook, letter to author, 8 March 1994.

7. Dinota.

8. Eiselein, letter.

9. Don Rinker, letter to author, 2 September 1993.

10. Janet Sauer, telephone interview by author, 12 January 1994.

11. Bob Rawls, letter to author, 12 October 1993.

12. Maria, letter, 6 November 1994.

13. Sommer, letter, 6 January 1994.

14. Grame, p. 89.

15. Michael Villalobos, letter to author, 16 December 1993.

16. Phoebe Nez, letter to author, 17 October 1993.

17. Nan Rubin, pp. 7–8.

18. Maria, letter, 6 November 1993.

19. Eiselein, letter.

20. Stu Schader, letter to author, 19 December 1993.

21. Telephone interview, Ray Cook, 27 November 1993.

22. Peter Tuluk, letter to author, 12 January 1994.

23. Rinker, letter, 24 September 1993.

24. Dinota.

25. Coffey.

26. Eiselein, letter.

27. Phoebe Nez, letter to author, 14 October 1993.

28. Nan Rubin, pp. 9, 16–17.

29. Cook, "Final Interim Report, p. 3.

30. Maria, letter, 6 November 1993.

31. Camille Lacapa-Morrison, letter to author, 26 August 1993.

32. Nan Rubin, p. 7.

33. Bob Rawls, letter to author, 7 October 1993.

34. Rinker, letter, 24 September 1993.

35. Stu Schader, letter to author, 8 January 1994.

36. Stu Schader, letter to author, 12 January 1994.

37. Duane Chimoni, letter to author, 6 October 1993.

38. Allen Myers, telephone interview by author, 20 December 1993.

39. Duane Chimoni, letter to author, 14 November 1993.

40. Ellis.

41. Chadwick.

## CHAPTER 7

1. Alex Looking Elk, telephone interview by author, 4 March 1994.

2. Stu Schader, letter to author, 6 December 1993.

3. Looking Elk.

4. A. J. S. Rayl, "New Technologies, Ancient Cultures," *Omni*, August 1993, p. 48.

5. Charles Trimble, letter to author, 3 March 1994.

6. Rick Hill in Eiselein, *Indian Issues*, p. 85.

7. Trimble.

8. Phoebe Nez, letter to author, 8 October 1993.

9. Coffey.

10. Peter Tuluk, letter to author, 7 November 1993.

11. Sommer, letter, 6 January 1994.

12. Duane Chimoni, telephone interview, 12 December 1993.

13. Maria, letter, 6 November 1993.

14. AIROS Operations Council proposal, 1992, p. 6.

15. Ibid., p. 7.

16. Ibid., p. 8.

17. Cook, letter to author, 14 March 1994.

18. Susan Braine, letter to author, 5 April 1994.

19. Cook, letter to author, 21 October 93.

20. Charles Trimble, Address to ICA, January 1994.

21. Goldberg. Paragraphing added.

22. Cook, letter, 8 March 1994.

23. Rinker, letter, 24 September 1993.

24. Ellis.

25. Trimble, Address.

26. Vince Two Eagles, letter to author, 30 November 1993.

27. Alex Looking Elk, telephone interview by author, 21 March 1994.

28. Trimble, Address.

# Further Reading

Brandon, William. *Indians*. Boston: Houghton-Mifflin, 1989.

Ceram, C. W. *The First Americans*. New York: Harcourt Brace Jovanovich, 1971.

Cornell, Stephen. *The Return of the Native*. New York: Oxford University Press, 1988.

David, Jay, ed. *The American Indian: The First Victim*. New York: William Morrow & Co., 1972.

Debo, Angie. *A History of the Indian of the United States*. Norman: University of Oklahoma Press, 1970.

Deloria, Vine, Jr., ed. *God Is Red*. New York: Grosset & Dunlap, 1973.

————, ed. *Of Utmost Good Faith*. San Francisco: Straight Arrow Books, 1971.

Edmunds, R. David, ed. *American Indian Leaders: Studies in Diversity*. Lincoln: University of Nebraska Press, 1980.

Fitzhugh, William W., ed. *Cultures in Contact*. Washington, D.C.: Smithsonian Institution Press, 1985.

Forbes, Jack D. *Black Africans and Native Americans*. Oxford: Basil Blackwell, 1988.

Fritz, Henry E. *The Movement of Indian Assimilation, 1860–1890*. Philadelphia: University of Pennsylvania Press, 1963.

Giago, Tim. *Notes from Indian Country*. Vol. 1. Pierre, S. D.: State Publishing Co., 1984.

Gooderham, Kent, ed. *I Am an Indian*. Toronto: J. M. Dent & Sons, 1969.

Hamilton, Charles. *Cry of the Thunderbird: The Indian's Own Story*. New York: Macmillan, 1950.

Head, Sydney W., Christopher H. Sterling, and Lemuel B. Schofield. *Broadcasting in America*. 7th ed. Boston: Houghton-Mifflin, 1994.

Hertzberg, Hazel W. *The Search for an American Indian Identity*. Syracuse: Syracuse University Press, 1971.

Hilliard, Robert L. and Michael C. Keith. *The Broadcast Century*. Stoneham, Mass.: Focal Press, 1992.

Jacobs, Wilbur R. *Dispossessing the American Indian*. New York: Charles Scribner's Sons, 1972.

Josephy, Alvin M., ed. *Red Power: The American Indian's Fight for Freedom*. New York: McGraw-Hill Book Co., 1972.

Katz, Jane B. *Let Me Be a Free Man*. Minneapolis: Lerner Publishing Co., 1975.

Kehoe, Alice B. *North American Indians: A Comprehensive Account*. Englewood Cliffs, N.J.: Prentice-Hall, 1981.

Mathiessen, Peter. *Indian Country*. New York: Viking Press, 1984.

Murphy, James, and Sharon Murphy. *Let My People Know*. Norman: University of Oklahoma Press, 1981.

O'Brien, Sharon. *American Indian Tribal Governments*. Norman: University of Oklahoma Press, 1989.

Olson, James S., and Raymond Wilson. *Native Americans in the Twentieth Century*. Urbana: University of Illinois Press, 1984.

Petrone, Penny, ed. *First People, First Voices*. Toronto: University of Toronto Press, 1983.

Prucha, Francis Paul. *The Great Father: The United States Government and the American Indian*. Lincoln: University of Nebraska Press, 1984.

Spicer, Edward H. *The American Indians: Dimensions of Ethnicity*. Cambridge: Harvard University Press, 1982.

Steiner, Stan. *The New Indians*. New York: Dell Publishing, 1968.

Thornton, Russell. *American Indian Holocaust and Survival*. Norman: University of Oklahoma Press, 1987.

Washburn, Wilcomb E., ed. *History of Indian-White Relations*. Vol. 4. Washington, D.C.: Smithsonian Institution Press, 1988.

Weatherford, Jack. *Native Roots: How the Indians Enriched America*. New York: Crown Publishers, 1991.

Weeks, Philip. *The American Indian Experience*. Arlington Heights, Il.: Forum Press, 1988.

# Index

**About the Author**

MICHAEL C. KEITH is a member of the Communication Department at Boston College. He is the author of several books on electronic media, including *The Radio Station* (3rd edition, 1993) and *The Broadcast Century: A Biography of American Broadcasting* (1992), with Robert Hilliard. He has held various positions at several radio stations, and was Chair of Education at the Museum of Broadcast Communications.